LET GO

Conquer Your Fear
Without Quitting

TORBEN RIF

LIFESTYLE
ENTREPRENEURS
P R E S S
LAS VEGAS, NV

ISBN: 978-1-946697-9-67

Published by:
Lifestyle Entrepreneurs Press
Las Vegas, NV

If you are interested in publishing through Lifestyle Entrepreneurs Press, write to: *Publishing@LifestyleEntrepreneursPress.com*

To learn more about our publications or about foreign rights acquisitions of our catalogue books, please visit: *www.LifestyleEntrepreneursPress.com*

Printed in the USA

"If there is no enemy within, the enemy outside can do us no harm."

— African proverb

This book is dedicated to Kamilla and Daniel, my two fantastic children:

You have taught me more than you can ever imagine.

I hope that I—with this book—can give you even more inspiration to listen to your bodies, follow your hearts, and create the lives you deserve.

Let no one tell you that you cannot achieve your dreams. Not even yourselves!

"The Way appears before the One that follows the heart."

— Dad

TABLE OF CONTENTS

PREFACE

By Rasmus Bengtsen, MA Chinese Studies

To Lose Face in China

"Man cannot live without face.
Trees cannot live without their bark."
(Chinese proverb)

Face isn't taken lightly in Chinese culture. The word "face" in this proverb is, of course, not about a person's physical appearance, but a reflection of pride, dignity, and stature in the eyes of the world around him. The expression "to lose face" in English actually comes from the Chinese expression "diu mianzi."

In China, "face" means a lot more than it does in the West. Many who come to China might think that the Chinese are overly sensitive. But in truth, losing face in China is a very serious, stigmatizing matter. In comparison to the rather harsh tone that one would experience in their interactions with Danes, one would observe that the Chinese tiptoe around one another. Just being contradicted at a social gathering can, to them, be considered a loss of face, and not being aware of this might cost you a friendship.

The importance of reputation is weighted differently in every society, but the current TV phenomenon *The X Factor* clearly illustrates the difference between the Chinese and Westerners. In the Chinese version of *The X Factor*, a lot of time is spent caring for the ego of the looser; just as the harsh Simon Cowell type is much milder in China. There exists ingrained aversion to losing face—not only in losing one's own face but also in causing another to lose face.

Just as you can win face through victories and successes, you can lose face by failing. Many Western leaders in China have come to realize that their employees will quit if criticized in front of their colleagues. They would simply rather be unemployed that live with the loss of face.

It cannot be overestimated how important the concept of face is in a hierarchical society like that of the Chinese. A serious loss of face is equal to a serious drop down the social ladder, and one will do whatever it takes in order to avoid it.

INTRODUCTION

The purpose of the book is to help people break the habits and beliefs that prevent them from living the life they dream about. Many detrimental beliefs that people have created are connected to experiences in the past.

Everything we've been through has made us what we are today, both good and bad. Whatever we have experienced, it has taught us something about how life is—what we can and cannot say, think, or do. Because these are only beliefs, however, they can be changed.

My goal is to give people who feel trapped or stuck some practical tools that they can use to change beliefs that have become obstacles to achieving their goals. With these tools, they can move towards a life where they are true to themselves, where they don't stop, no matter what others say and think about them, and where they follow their hearts.

I wrote this book because, for many years—most of my life, really—I felt trapped in a pattern where I have struggled to maintain the ego and the facade I had built up. I have certainly been successful in many areas, but at the same time I have suffered from low self-esteem and beliefs that I wasn't good enough.

My dream is that other people experience the same freedom that I experienced when I LET GO. It's the wildest feeling to have the courage and the strength to be myself, to stand up and show myself as I am, no matter what others may say or think.

I do not have a recognized education, and I am not a therapist or psychologist, nor do I boast having magic tools for success, but I have studied, trained, and taught in Chinese martial arts for more than 30 years. I have worked with people most of my life and worked as a kind of coach and supervisor for thousands of students over the years.

I have taught business leaders and their employees in this Chinese philosophy and strategy for more than 20 years— primarily for conflict resolution, communication, and for the purpose of LETTING GO and being present. I have taught them in the art of overcoming their fears without giving up, as well as the art of achieving their goals, no matter what.

I have had my own business since 1994 and continue to run a successful business where I lecture and train instructors in Wudang tai chi chuan and qigong.

Let Go

THE KEY IS PRACTICE: WUDANG TAI CHI CHUAN

LET GO is based on my own life experiences and my long career with Chinese martial arts, especially Wudang tai chi chuan. I started like many others in my generation with karate and the toughest type of martial arts in the military. I have always been fascinated by martial arts, and Bruce Lee was my role model.

What is Wudang tai chi chuan?

Tai chi chuan is a Chinese martial art that is best known for its slow, aesthetic movements. Why is it that we move so slowly? It's like we've almost stopped and cannot move faster.

Wudang is the name of this style, and we use this name to recognize Chang San-Feng as the founder of tai chi chuan. He lived in the Wudang Mountains in China. There are many different styles, and even though each style does the techniques a bit differently, our basic goal is the same: inner peace, harmony, and balance.

7

There are many reasons why we move slowly.

Here are some of the most important, from my point of view: As we move very slowly and breathe through the nose with the mouth closed, then the lungs will expand down instead of out, meaning, according to the Chinese, we get deeper and longer breathing, which means we get more oxygen (qi) into the body and to the cells. More oxygen to the cells means stronger health.

As we move slowly and relax as much as possible, without losing the body structure and technique, we work deeper into the muscles and strengthen their stabilizing components. There is an old saying that says, "When a tai chi master is standing, you cannot move him."

It has nothing to do with size and strength but how the master uses the different parts of the body as one, especially the stabilizing part of the muscles.

The keys to a good foundation, both physically and mentally, are the more mysterious exercises called nei gung. Nei gung means internal strength, and the exercises direct us to work inside and out—we build the body from within rather than all the superficial work we see in some other forms of training.

> *"Without gung, martial
> art is waste of time."*
> Chinese proverb

It requires both physical and mental strength to live with all the challenges we face in everyday life, and nei gung is my way of creating this foundation. The exercises are a kind of qigong (energy work), just better. The complete set consists of 24 exercises: one set of 12 yin exercises and one set of 12 yang exercises. Each set takes about an hour to complete and will give you a great foundation.

You must have some foundation before learning these exercises, and therefore, it takes typically a year before you are allowed to "walk inside the door" and learn them. They are not secret but are reserved for dedicated students, students who really are interested in strengthening their health both physically and mentally and are also capable of providing the effort it requires.

The key to a life in balance is practice and daily exercise, both physically and mentally. Wudang tai chi chuan, qigong, and the tools in this book can help us provide a solid foundation so we are even better equipped when we meet challenges and resistance.

MY STORY

We are on the plane to London. It is 1998, and I'm on my way to the British Open Tai Chi Championship with my students. The mood is great, and we're ready! This time I'm not competing; I'm there only to coach and lend support to my students, who have been practicing diligently and are focused for this event.

We're talking and swapping stories from earlier competitions. I can feel the desire to compete; it's really pulling at me. Even though I haven't prepared, I have been practicing every single day. So I'm thinking that I could easily compete and win. I have done so before. My thoughts are telling me, *No, Torben. Not this time. This time you are here for the sake of your students.*

We arrive at the hotel, and I'm still absorbed in my thoughts of competing. I don't get much sleep that night because I'm lying there imagining what winning would be like. As the morning comes, I choose to ignore my previous decision: *Of course, I'm competing!* I tell myself confidently. And I'm going to complete in my two favorite disciplines: fixed step and moving step push hands. Fixed step is a discipline in which you are not allowed to move your feet. If you do, your opponent scores points. Moving step is a discipline in which you typically move within an arena of four-by-four meters. Here you attempt to get your opponent either down on the floor or out of the arena. Pushing hands is a sort of balance wrestling match in which two persons practice and test their close-quarter abilities.

The competition starts, and as it becomes my turn, I can feel the excitement rise. But I'm on top of this. I keep seeing myself being cheered, applauded, and envied. I am ready.

The opponent taking his place in front of me is a young and strong man. Even though he looks at least as ready as I am, he is still just a kid. He doesn't have the experience that I do. He knows nothing about...

The next thing I remember is flying out of the arena to land heavily on my shoulder.

In total shock, I'm lying there thinking, *Hello, Torben! Are you awake!? This guy is serious!* I get up again and come in contact with the kid. But it does not take long before I again land on the mats outside the arena.

This is not good. I can feel the wondering stares from my students, who—like myself—do not really comprehend what is going on. I just know that I don't stand a chance! I have to do something.

I get up on one knee and grab my shoulder, suddenly feeling a lot of pain. *"It is that old injury come back,"* I say, while clenching my eyes shut for all to see how painful it is. I cannot continue. Not with this shoulder.

And so, "reluctantly," I withdrew from the match and let the kid win.

Deep down inside, I knew very well that I had never been ready for that match. But my pride was so great that I had to feign an injury in order not to disappoint my students. Rather than paying my opponent respect for having practiced and for his martial abilities, I pretended that my injury was worse that it truly was. This gave me the opportunity to withdraw without the loss of face.

That ability I developed very early in my life.

AN INSECURE, CONFIDENT KID

I never forgot the sound of the wind in the trees, the many-meters-high poplars, rising tall at the end of our garden, the fresh air of the countryside, and the animals on our little farm. I rode a horse before I could walk.

I was born in Herlev but grew up in Sakskoebing on Lolland in the southern part of Denmark. We had a smallholding with 10 acres of land. Here my father grew corn and sugar beets as a sort of hobby farmer besides his full time job as a police officer. At home, my mother took care of us three boys, which was probably much the same as a full time job or more.

My brothers and I grew up in a healthy and harmonic home, unlike my parents, who both grew up among arguments and violence. They had undoubtedly experienced many things in their childhoods that no child should experience. Luckily for us, they had decided that they wanted to deviate from their social heritage and make sure that we three boys didn't share those experiences. And we didn't. We had a good and safe foundation on which to build our lives.

My father was a great role model. He wasn't the type to take shortcuts—ever. When he did something, he did his very best. He expected the same from the rest of us. It was true for everything, even the smallest of things, like when I had made a drawing. It was not important that I had done a good job; what was important was that the drawing could be better. The challenge was that everything could be better. Always.

For this reason, the appreciative pats on the back were few and far between. But, of course, it only made me try even harder and do everything even better in order to get his recognition. I just had to do everything perfectly or be the best, and then I would get that extra dose of attention.

I therefore started very early to define myself by how perfectly I could DO things. I did my best to avoid making mistakes.

My way of defining myself was a challenge at school. Academically, I was not particularly strong. I was not bad, but I was far from being the best. Combined with a complete lack of interest, I had a hard time. I fought a constant battle not to make any mistakes.

I very quickly learned that if I gave a wrong answer or made a mistake, the other students would laugh and tease me afterwards. They might not have been laughing at me, but at what I said or did. No matter what, I still took it personally, and didn't feel accomplished enough.

I did feel accomplished, however, when I played soccer in the breaks between classes.

Sports became my rescue

From the first moment I stood between the goal posts, I knew that soccer was something I was good at. That is why I started playing soccer at a very young age. Here I could perform, and I got a lot of praise and recognition.

As goalkeeper for the boys, junior, and youth teams, I soon became the key player. "Unfortunately," this meant I had to "live with" a lot of praise from my coach and fellow players. But every now and then, however rarely it happened, if anyone criticized me, I came close to giving up. Giving it all up and dropping the sport. I was devastated if anyone criticized me, and I took it very personally. The only thing that kept me going was all the praise I got, as I was actually very good at soccer and people talked about me possessing a huge talent.

My father had always taught me that I should aim higher and stick to it. I was extremely proud of the club and my first team. I looked up to Palle, who was the best goalkeeper in the club.

I trained hard and prioritized soccer. Dreams of the national team were beginning to take shape. But before getting there, I had to pass through to the first team. I often caught myself daydreaming about the day when I would keep goal for the first team every Sunday—at the town stadium with lots of spectators. And the day was closer than I had imagined.

One day, the first team's goalkeeper, Palle, was injured. And the coach decided that he would rather use me for the coming, important match than the reserve goalkeeper. As you can imagine, I was extremely proud!

BUT...

I could also feel how my fear of failing suddenly took over as he told me that the media would be present. The media!

As the day dawned, I was really nervous and couldn't focus at all.

The coach and team leader was worried and pulled me into the office before we went onto the field. We had a good chat, and the team leader finished the chat by pulling out a bottle of Danish bitter, Gammel Dansk. I had a couple of shots and calmed down somewhat. At least on the outside. Inside I was still dying of fright!

The game began, and I actually felt pretty good. Whether it was my confidence or the shots had started working, I have no idea. The most important thing was that I had calmed down and felt on top of things. The score was 0-0 at halftime, and we were doing well in the game. 20 minutes into the second half, the opponents had a corner, and we prepared to defend.

At 176 centimeters, I was not the tallest goalkeeper in the world, but I was fast as lightning and could jump high and quick. I was in the zone, even though the fear of making a mistake was still lurking.

The kick was made, the ball was coming, and I made a quick decision: *I am going to take that!* I yelled as loud as I could: "I GOT IT!" and jumped for it. But I had misjudged the distance! Shortly after, I saw how the ball flew light and elegant right over my fingertips, and on towards the goal. *No way! Oh no!* I closed my eyes and imagined how every spectator in the crowd would look at me and blame me.

It was as if I saw myself from the outside, lying there, fumbling around on the grass, while the opponents effortlessly kicked the ball into the net. I imagined pictures of me on the front cover of the newspaper the next day with the heading: *"Major screw-up by the new goalkeeper: It's all Torben's fault!"*

Before I could start visualizing my father's disappointment, I heard the roar of the crowd. Our "defensive rock" had saved us on the line! *"GET UP, TORBEN! WE GOT THE BALL!"* he yelled at me. Confused, I got on my feet, looked around, straightened my back, and showed the audience that I had been in control the whole time.

My abilities in cheating

In ninth grade, we arrived at the obligatory point at which we had to decide what we wanted to do after graduating school. All my classmates had a fair idea about it, but I didn't have a clue. I had been with the police and the military as an intern for a short while in school, and both were very exciting. I could easily see myself wearing a uniform on a daily basis.

But I was too young to apply for either the police or the military. So I chose to follow the current into college, where I could stay until my uniform was ready for me.

Before college, my entire focus had been on my hobbies, such as soccer, handball, gymnastics, and badminton. I soon realized that I wouldn't have time for all that if I also had to do my homework. And homework became a major challenge for me. Not only because I felt I could not keep up, but also because they meant that I had to give up on all the things that really gave me energy and recognition. After all, I had been living for my hobbies and the recognition that followed.

In college, I struggled to not lose face. I was constantly struggling to keep up. My interests were elsewhere, and I did not have "time" to do my assignments or prepare for my classes.

I had to find a way where I could get through the day without losing face, so I would make excuses daily, like "I forgot my work at home" or something similar. That way I did not have to present anything, and nobody could see how bad I was—at least, that's how I saw it. It was a terrible time, a constant struggle to "survive" and to maintain the facade.

Several of the classes, physics in particular, were gibberish to me. I really didn't understand much of what was being said. So I made sure to be pals with those that did. This way I had someone to copy papers from. It worked, and I got good grades. So I had more time for my hobbies.

This is how it went for several months, and even though nobody had found out, I knew deep down inside that it was only a matter of time. My down-prioritizing of school and homework had left me far behind the others, and I was in deep waters. In a few months we were going to the exams, and then everyone would find out that I wasn't as good as they thought.

I had to find a way that I could get out of college without losing face. I had to find a story that would work with my parents.

What to do?

One morning, we sat around the breakfast table, and I told my parents that I needed to talk with them. I had had a bellyache for several days and was mega nervous about telling them that I wanted to quit college. I told them that I did not have the drive to continue in college, I could not see myself using it for anything, and I had run completely weary of it. So I wanted to stop.

To my great surprise, they took it nicely and asked what I wanted to do. "I want to be a soldier!" I said immediately.

"Okay," said my father. "Then figure out how to get in. And in the meantime, you need something to do. So how about asking Joern Erik Kaare, on one of the bigger farms nearby, if he might need a helping hand?" That very afternoon I drove over to Joern Erik, and shortly after, I had a full time farming job.

I had "forgotten" to tell my parents that I had been cheating most of my way through the first semester of college.

The Special Forces and my wake-up call

After eight months with Joern Erik, I was finally on my way to Oksboel where I was to start as a soldier. When I walked around on my first day and looked at all the soldiers in their uniforms, I remember fantasizing about how many stars I'd get on *my* uniform.

I believe I had only been a soldier for about a year and a half when a very special poster appeared on the note board: *Tryouts for the Special Forces!*

Once in college we had a visit by a genuine Special Forces Operator, who had filled the gymnasium with adrenaline-hungry boys. We all sat there watching as this impressive man came walking down through the rows. Stars on his shoulders and all kinds of decorations on his shirt—probably from all the secret missions he had been on. Damn, he looked good! I was hooked! On that day I decided that if I ever got the opportunity, I wanted to join the Special Forces.

Now I had that opportunity! I didn't think much about it and just applied in a hurry. This was my calling!

The Special Forces was the elite, and now I was going. I trained like a madman in order to pass the admittance demands. The preliminary tests went well, and I was ready to go for the Special Forces candidate course.

Fifty-four of us came to the base in Aalborg. Among us, there were five SAS soldiers from England, the English Special Forces; they were said to be extremely tough—and they were. We were well received, and everybody was friendly on the evening we arrived. The tone was quite different, however, when we fell in on Monday morning at the training grounds. There was yelling and screaming—as if taken straight from an American war movie.

The preliminary tests that we had been through just to get here were up again. But where we earlier had had an entire week for them, we now only had two days! That set the standard.

The first test was the bronze circle training, which is a calisthenics program with pull-ups, push-ups, crunches, and jumping jacks. We were to go through it three times in less than 12 minutes, just as we had done before. The difference was that this time there was a real Special Forces operator with each of us to count our repetitions. I do not know how any of the others felt, but I had a problem concentrating with this superhero standing there.

But the tests went well. Actually, more than well. I did it in nine minutes, which was three minutes faster than demanded. I already felt like one of them as the Special Force operator came and gave me the time. I had expected that he would high five me or pat me on the shoulder to recognize my top form. But he didn't even react. He just noted the time and turned around.

Shortly after, it was time for the run. 2400 meters that had to be completed in less than 12 minutes. *This should not be a problem. It's just a matter of finding the pace and doing what it takes*, I thought. The route was 800 meters and therefore had to be run three times. The first couple of laps went well. My pace was okay, and I wasn't as hard pressed as I had feared. But on the third lap I felt the impact that the calisthenics had left in my legs. They started to feel heavy and weren't as willing anymore. I could feel a fear was rising in me. *Is this where I will be sent home? On the first day?* With my thoughts racing and heavy legs, I crossed the line in 11:54...

The self-confidence test

The first week progressed with one test after another. We weren't only pressed physically, but very much mentally as well! The operators cursed, yelled at, and degraded us all day long.

One day we were going through a series of self-confidence tests in the pool area. One of them was to jump from the three-meter tower blindfolded. I got up there, had a bag put over my head, and asked for permission to perform the self-confidence test. I got permission and jumped. No problem.

But in the afternoon it was time for one of the "big" self-confidence tests: jumping from the parachute tower. We had heard a great deal about the famous tower and looked forward to it with mixed emotions. As we saw it for the first time, it did not appear that special. I was thinking, *I got this. I can handle this.* But as we got closer, it was as if the tower grew and grew. *This cannot be,* I thought. *It cannot keep growing...*

Close to tower we all gathered. We had been 54 to begin with, but we were already down to 35. Most of us looked quite nervously at this tower. Damn, it was tall. "This tower is 18 meters high," the Special Forces instructor in front of us yelled. "This is the self-confidence test number five. The rules are simple: You jump, and you continue. You do not, and you go home."

Shortly after, we—one by one—started climbing the 18-meter-high tower. I did not know there could be THIS many steps in such a tower... They just kept going on and on. Slowly, one by one, the others started jumping. Every now and then, a clearly disappointed person who had not had the courage to jump came down the stairs. They got sent home. *This might not be as simple as I had imagined,* I thought to myself.

My turn was coming up. I had reached the top and could now see what was going on. One by one, we put on the harness and prepared to jump. In front of me was a guy named Dan, and I could see that he was not well. None of us really were. The difference was just that Dan was one of those guys who was always in the top, no matter what we had done. He was one of those that the rest of us looked up to.

As it became his turn, and he had prepared himself, he called for permission to jump. The Special Forces instructor at the base of the tower yelled, "PERMISSION GRANTED." But Dan didn't jump. He hesitated and stayed where he was. He was once again given permission, but still just stood there. It was clear that they could see potential in Dan because they gave him much more time than any of the others. "PERMISSION GRANTED," the Special Forces instructor called for the last time. But there was nothing to do. Dan, the toughest among us all, was being sent home right before my eyes. And now it was my turn...

I could feel my legs shaking as I slowly walked over to the edge; my head was swarming with thoughts. I didn't want to go home now, but I didn't want to die either. So, as I stood there, ready to jump, I started contemplating the advantages and disadvantages of either going home or dying. I decided to take my chances and asked for permission to jump.

"PERMISSION GRANTED" the Special Forces Instructor yelled.

I leaned out and jumped.

In the five-meter free fall before the lines were extended, I saw a lot of pictures of my life. I really thought I was about to die. But the lines held me, and together we just floated down, the steel wires hanging horizontally from the tower and out to a hillock 40 meters away. I was in a state of euphoria, which I believe many will recognize from overcoming something great! Less than a minute before, I was comparing life to death, almost writing my last will and testament, and soiling my underwear! Now I sat there and felt like going again! Luckily that wasn't an option, and it was a far more pressing matter to get back and change said underwear.

With my pride intact

A few days later, in the late morning, the whole crew walked like a group of zombies towards the pool area. We had been out walking the whole day before and running an orienteering at night. It felt like we hadn't slept in several years.

In the night's orienteering I had gotten lost and ended up not finding a single post. After having been running around for a couple of hours in the dark woods, I finally found my way back to the trucks that were to drive us back to barracks. Here one of the Special Forces instructors received me with a very strict face: "Where the hell have you been? How many posts did you find?"

"None," I had to admit, after which he completely freaked out on me and ended up giving me a bonus of 20 push-ups and jumping jacks.

On the way back in the truck, we were shivering as if it was a competition and our teeth were clacking. We were wet and tired, pressed to the limit after the past two weeks of unending tests. The sun was coming up, and we were just looking forward to getting back to the barracks for a hot shower. And a lot of sleep. But we were barely off the truck before a Special Forces instructor appeared. "EVERYBODY FALL IN AT THE POOL AREA IN TWO— READY FOR SWIMMING IN UNIFORM, BOOTS, AND SUBMACHINEGUN!"

We all looked resignedly at each other. At the same time, I could feel my body starting to give in. I felt like I had been run over by a steamroller. My head was heavy, all my muscles were dead, and the exertion of the night had left me with a fever.

As I finally got in the water at the pool area, the trouble started coming in. After only a few laps, I was having trouble keeping my head above water. I knew what I was supposed to do, but my body just couldn't move. I literally fought to keep above water. But finally I had to give in and fought my way to the side of the pool. The Special Forces instructor who walked along the pool spotted me and immediately came running towards me—while spewing forth every curse known in the Danish language. But as he approached me, he recognized that I was a mess.

With snot pouring out my nose, fiery red eyes, and a face as white as chalk, it was obvious that I was seriously ill. He pulled me from the water and instructed me to report to the doctor. The doctor recommended I stay in bed for the next five days and get plenty of rest. Funny enough, that was exactly what I felt the most like doing.

Shortly after, I was called to the office where four of the instructors were waiting for me. As I saw them I thought, *Shit—now I'm in for it!* But no, they spoke politely and almost caringly. The chief said that he had no doubt that I was a mess and that they didn't wish play roulette with my health. That's why they thought it best that I take the five days in bed, as recommended by the doctor, and come back fresh.

But deep inside, I could feel that I was out of my depth. It would have been only a matter of time before I would have failed one test or another anyway. I was nowhere near in the shape needed to pass.

I, thinking quickly, argued to them that I would have a really hard time catching up if I was gone for a week. They conferred shortly and (luckily) ended with acknowledging my argument. They commended me for my dedication and effort and my responsible way of thinking. The encounter seemed to alleviate my fever somewhat. The conference ended with them giving me a note, which said that I had to stop due to illness but was welcome to return for another try.

The truth was that, yes, I got ill, but probably wouldn't have made it anyway. I was nowhere near mentally strong enough to handle this. Both my body and my mind knew that it was very unlikely that I would give another try.

On the other hand, that little piece of paper meant that I could go back to my old barracks with my pride intact. And so I did.

After a week horizontal, I was shipped back, where I, of course, had to endure comments about me not making it. Naturally I didn't tell them that I had nearly quit on my own. I just showed them the paper, and then they relented.

Luckily no one knew the real truth. And, throughout the five years I spent in the army, that paper was pulled forth regularly. And instead of losing face, I got loads of respect and recognition. Exactly as I wanted it.

The old Chinese man

As a professional soldier, self-defense and physical martial arts were things that I practiced a lot. Martial arts had fascinated me since I was a child, which is why I decided on my return home to seek out the local martial arts club. I wanted to start having regular weekly practice. I was usually stronger than the others and really felt on top. The martial practice was the height of my day.

We practiced a mix of boxing and karate, but without the traditional self-defense techniques. All focus was on strength and fighting practice, and I loved it. Mostly because I was one of the best.

One day, as we arrived for practice, there was an old Chinese man moving in slow motion. We gave it a look, laughed a little, and thought that he'd be done by the time we started. But he wasn't.

Our instructor had invited him, and he was to teach us something called tai chi that evening. We weren't thrilled, but we had enough respect for our instructor to go along with it. The Chinese man soon felt that we weren't much interested in his slow movements, so he took a look around and told us that he needed a volunteer.

As the only one in class who trained in a sleeveless t-shirt—so you could see my muscles—his eyes fell on me. He asked me step forward. With his 160 centimeters and "fighting weight" of about 50 kilos, he didn't seem like much as he stood there before me.

"HIT ME," he instructed. I stepped slowly forward and carefully struck out at him. I didn't want to hurt the old man. But, before I knew it, he punched me right in the head so I went down. While lying there, he just looked down at me and said: "Are you going to get up, boy?"

Senior citizen or not, he was in for it now. I quickly got up again and intended to hit him with full force. But all I hit was air, and he, moments later, proceeded to throw me around the gym. I flew into the walls, down on the floor, and over into the faces of the others. I quickly got up again and tried to hit him even harder and faster. But the harder I punched, the farther I flew—to the great enjoyment of the rest of the class.

This infuriated me so badly; I felt like I was about to explode. I could also feel how I—in step with my frustration—made more and more mistakes. It was as if the more I tried, the worse it got. The Chinese man smiled, and the others laughed. In the end, I struck out so hard at him that my overexertion of force made me slip and fall over my own feet—without him even touching me. Everybody was laughing, and my own instructor stopped this "uneven" match. I gave the old Chinese man a crooked smile, but inside I was in a crisis about what had just happened. I had just been severely humiliated by a small, old man who could throw me around with ease—in spite of my 100 kilos of muscle and towering self-confidence.

Afterwards I laughed along with the others and told them that, of course, I hadn't done my best. "He was, after all, an old man, and I didn't want to hurt him" was my conclusion. Luckily, I was very skilled at hiding my insecurity and frustration, so everyone believed it. I had my pride intact.

Just up until the day when I met a man who saw right through me.

Meeting my master

At the end of 1990, as we were about finished with a training session, I saw someone posting a flyer in the fitness center. *Tai Chi for Beginners* it read, and the picture showed a man lying on his back while another man jumped from a height of two meters down on his stomach. *Cool*, I thought. It looked interesting. Even though I still tried to avoid conversations about my debut with tai chi and the old Chinese man, it had still fascinated me. *Imagine if I was the guy who could toss around big, grown-up men in that way.* So I chose to go and took a trial lesson.

The chief instructor of the club, Brian, received us at the Noerremarkens School in Vejle. He was about my height and very muscular. He started with telling us that he was a black belt in five different martial arts and had practiced tai chi in London with the master himself.

The training went well, and I quickly caught on to the techniques. It felt quite natural to me, as I could use my strength to toss around most of the students. And yes, it didn't take many evenings of training before I was even able to toss around the instructor too. I started to sense that I had found a martial art with which I really felt at home.

I had not practiced more than four months when Brian's master came to Denmark and for the first time held a weekend seminar of tai chi. Brian had told us so much about him and praised him highly, so we were, of course, very excited.

The master, after graduating in karate in the early '70s, had gone to Hong Kong to find a tai chi master who knew how to use tai chi as a martial art, which wasn't all that easy.

He had found several in Europe who taught the slow part of tai chi but none who knew the martial art behind tai chi. The master had gotten a job with the Hong Kong Royal Police and through connections there had found Grandmaster

Cheng Tinhung, who taught practical tai chi chuan. He practiced several times a week with this master, who was one of the foremost masters in Hong Kong.

After about nine years in Hong Kong and the Southeastern Championships of Full Contact, he became one of the top students. And in agreement with his master, he decided to go back to Europe to spread this style called Wudang tai chi chuan—practical tai chi chuan.

The master landed a few days before the seminar was to be held, as it was his first visit to Denmark. This meant that he came and oversaw our weekly training, which we had two days before the weekend.

We were at our weekly practice, and he just sat and watched us quietly. The practice included, among others, self-defense techniques and pushing hands. I was totally fascinated with pushing hands, which is a form of balance wrestling. This also meant that I rather quickly caught on to the idea of it, so that even Brian had trouble tumbling me.

We were close to the end of the training, and we did pushing hands in pairs. I excelled at it, turning over everyone, including my instructor Brian, who I pushed over time and again. The master, who had been sitting quietly and studying us, got up with his more than 190 centimeters and came over to us. "May I have a try?" he asked nicely and quietly. Of course, he could, even though I was a bit nervous about what was about to happen. Shortly after he had put his huge hands on my huge arms, which to my great surprise, didn't seem that huge anymore, they were completely locked, and I couldn't move them.

As soon as I started trying to wrest free, he changed direction, which meant that I flew away, without him using any force. Time and again I flew off into the walls, over at the others, or down on the floor. *Pull yourself together, Torben! You can do this!* I was thinking to myself. But no matter what I tried, he just tossed me around.

"You'll learn someday." He ended with a smile.

The following weekend with the master was absolutely fantastic. And it would be one of many great weekends that I had with him. We learned a great deal—both practically and theoretically. Among others, we learned the entire short square and round hand form, which is 34 techniques put together to form one long series, plenty of self-defense, and pushing hands, which would normally take about a year to learn. Okay, what we learned wasn't pretty, but we could remember it.

It would be about four years before the master again came to Denmark. This time it was me who had invited him.

Full of expectations, I stood in Billund Airport, ready to take him home to the former farmhouse where I lived with my wife at that time and my son Daniel. My master had arrived a few days before the seminar was to be held so I could get some private lessons with him.

It was like an old Kung Fu movie, where the student and teacher were together for several days. I was hugely excited. We started every day with nei kung, which consists of 24 exercises, 12 yin and 12 yang. And over the next two days, everything Brian had taught me through the first four years was being corrected in detail.

Those were some hard days, but just being with the master made me forget all about the pain that came with it. Even though I was used to training hard, I wasn't used to practicing eight hours a day. One form after another was corrected, and the techniques were examined. It was just fantastic, and I could feel myself improving every hour that went by.

The master was very patient and caring in his way of correcting my techniques. At the same time, he praised me and said that with my talent I could become one of the very best in the world. He made me feel so important, so special, and so good. I got the recognition I constantly hungered for. He was a world champion at making me feel good enough.

In the time after this fantastic weekend, I felt really good! My relationship with the master continued to develop. I participated in several camps and weekend seminars and even went over to London to spend time with him privately, where I stayed with for several days. He had really taken me under his wing and showed me the way, like a true master.

My way to becoming a master

I have always been driven by being the best, so when I was offered the opportunity to teach Wudang tai chi chuan, I accepted immediately. I had previously taught in gymnastics and had worked as a fitness instructor, so the teaching part was not unfamiliar to me.

At the same time, I saw the chance to get the role of teacher for others, and the title "chief instructor" provided recognition in and of itself. I felt comfortable in my role as manager of the local club, and it proved to be a way of life for me.

Did I have the ability to teach? Obviously. But did I possess the level of teaching necessary to take on this role? That's up for discussion. Many would probably say NO—that I should have had many years of experience before I started teaching others—and they may be right.

We stood in a situation where one of us had to take the class or the association would die because our instructor was going to move from town. I accepted the challenge, and it went very well.

From instructor to master

It was a long road to becoming a master, but it has also been an amazing journey. I grew with the task, and one club turned into many when my students became so skilled that they started their own clubs around Denmark.

I traveled around Europe to teach, and my skill level increased with every day that I taught. I trained hard to become the best and won one tournament after another. My teaching evolved to be much more than physical movements in slow motion; the Chinese philosophy gained more and more space in my teaching and in my own life.

When I started teaching, I felt like something special, but later the goal was to raise my students above myself, like my master had.

This is also why the disappointment was unbearable when my own master deliberately chose to humiliate me in front of all my students...

How could he do it?

We were on a summer camp in Sweden with the master as our teacher. It had been great, and at the time I was one of the most experienced of his students. This made me a sort of right hand or number two for many of the students. This status I wore with incredibly huge pride.

We had reached the last day of the camp, and we were working in various groups. I did a partner exercise with the spear along with Tony, who was the instructor of the local club. We went around in a circle, each with a spear. Our spears had to be in contact at all times, while we moved them in circles. We had been doing the exercise for some time when the master suddenly yelled, "STOP!" Everybody stopped and stared.

In a rage he yelled: "Torben and Tony, what the hell are you doing!? Do it again!" All 45 participants, mind you, those were Tony's and my students, stood stock-still and looked at this happening. "Do it again, and this time do it right!" the master yelled. None of us were entirely sure about what he meant, but we started over. It didn't take long before he stopped us. "If that's the best you can do, you should consider finding another hobby." The gym was completely silent, and we had no idea what he was on about.

"Now I'll show you how it's done." He took a spear and signaled at Tony to do the exercise with him. They started out, and I have to admit that I couldn't see the difference. "You're supposed to be chief instructors! The least one can expect should be for you to do it right. You must be down in the knees, not moving around up high like a couple of amateurs. Do it again!"

Now I was outraged, but I still did the exercise, ready to explode. I left the camp in Sweden that afternoon without uttering a single word to the master. This summer camp's final exercise would become a turning point that I hadn't seen coming.

He had humiliated me in front of all my students! How could he do that to me? I thought I was his right hand man. Why would he suddenly treat me like some fresh beginner?

My brother John, who was also at the camp, told me that maybe it was a test of loyalty towards the master. The Chinese generals had often tested the loyalty of their officers by giving them various challenges. *Hmm, did he really want to test my loyalty?* I had been loyal all the way and promoted him everywhere I went. Even though it made some sense to me, it didn't change the fact that I felt very sorry for myself...for several weeks.

The humiliations continued

Some time later, we were again gathered for the Wudang tai chi chuan summer camp at Skövde in Sweden. I had buried the last experience and was ready to go again. We were a gathering of 45 enthusiasts, both instructors and students, gathered for five days to be taught by the master.

There was always a fantastic energy at these gatherings, and it gave me a feeling of being part of something bigger than myself.

Over the five days, several of us were to take the so-called instructor's exam, which basically is about demonstrating certain techniques and explaining the theory behind them. It all went super well, and my turn was coming up. I was ready.

The day before, the master had asked me what level I believed I was. Of the nine levels there are, I thought myself to have reached level seven. He looked at me and said: "Okay, I will ask you about three things tomorrow, then we will see if you are level seven." That night I didn't sleep much because I was constantly worrying about what he might ask.

The next morning, we were ready for practice, but the master hadn't showed up yet. So we started with some warm-up exercises outside. While we were at it, a taxi suddenly came.

To our great surprise, the master jumped out of it, shirt buttoned crooked and his hair sticking out to all sides. Halfway between the taxi and us, he dumped his bag on the grass while yelling: "Torben, it's time! Self-defense single whip. Get started!"

The test had officially started. I was to teach all the participants the single whip technique, after which they paired up two by two and practiced it. The master disappeared into the office and came back 10 minutes later yelling, "NEXT!" I looked at him, puzzled by his almost dictator-like style and felt slightly insecure. But, of course, I did as he told me and showed the participants another variation of the same technique. He disappeared once more and came back again. "NEXT!" This time he just stood there staring at me while I was teaching. "NEXT!" And so, it kept going for about an hour, until I ran out of variations.

"I have no more," I told him.

He looked at me condescendingly, narrowing his eyes, and said, "OKAY! NOT PASSED. Next instructor."

What the heck is going on?! I was thinking, while boiling inside. In pure anger I left the field and threw the water bottle I had in my hand directly into an innocent tree. The bottle perished, while the tree got a little extra water that day. I walked around inside to let off some steam. Got back outside and sat down on the stairs of the clubhouse. Good thing it was the last day of the camp because I certainly wasn't going to participate anymore.

How could he do it again? What was it that he wanted to tell me? Why did he do it in front of my students? I had a lot of thoughts running through my head, and I felt really bad. *Why doesn't he like me anymore?*

One thing was certain. He had decided that I shouldn't pass that day—no matter what I said or did. That's how it was.

But I didn't have the courage to confront him about it. Instead I was just burning more and more. "Why do I put up with this treatment!?" I kept asking myself. But my answer always came to the fact that the master was the best at this style. And since I wanted to be the best, it was no use learning from the second best.

Despite all this, I still had a bellyache over his way of treating me. I had allowed him to step on me because I was afraid to stand up for myself. I was afraid of losing my master. I was afraid of losing his respect. And, even more importantly, his recognition.

But fate decided that I would lose him anyway.

I lost it!

Through the years, one of my most important ways to gain the acknowledgement of others and myself had been by collecting proof of my skills. Trophies. Medals. Diplomas. Certificates. Much in the same way that the little note from the Special Forces had helped tell others how tough I was.

So back when the master started certifying his instructors, it was obvious that I was going to aim for the absolute highest level: level 9. I wanted to be the best, and I wanted proof of it.

Year after year, I practiced like a madman and passed one level after another. When I finally passed level 8, the second highest, it was a huge win for me. I was now so very close to being one of the very best, and I had fought hard to get it. Very few people in the world had this status.

On one ordinary afternoon as I was working on my computer, an email popped up from one of the master's female students in Denmark. She just wanted to tell me that on that day she had passed her level 8 and had been appointed Chief Instructor of Wudang Tai Chi Chuan Denmark. Exactly the same as me.

I was in total shock! I knew her very well and knew that less than a day before, she had only been level 4! And now she was suddenly level 8. How was that possible?

I tried writing and calling the master several times in the following days but got no reply. What was going on? I spoke with some of my old students, who had been with me for years, and nobody understood. To exclude him pulling a joke on me, I visited the woman's homepage and had to conclude that it was true. I was stunned.

I went over and looked at my own certificate on the wall. I took it down, sat in my chair, and looked at it. I stared for a long time at this status symbol, which I had fought for so many years to get and that she had suddenly just been given. I was boiling inside, I ended up taking the certificate out of the frame and tearing it to pieces. If she could gain the same level, this certificate was worth nothing.

It felt as if I had been betrayed by my own master. The man, who I had faithfully and loyally followed for 17 years, had stepped on me for the last time. Now I could finally see how he had treated me through all these years. As the years had gone by, he had been more and more on my back, and it felt as if he tried to keep me down. The supportive and caring master had disappeared, and a cold, condescending dictator had taken his place.

That day, I decided to say goodbye to my master.

When I really lost face

In the time after, I didn't hold myself back from telling people how he had treated me. How I had been humiliated. How he had betrayed me by giving an inferior student the same level as me. I did everything I could to turn people to my side so I could justify cutting contact with him.

But it also left me in a situation, where I—whether I was justified or not—didn't feel as self-confident anymore. Whether I wanted it or not, the master's opinion through the years had been the foundation on which I had built my identity. It was his recognition and certificates that made me feel tough.

One Sunday afternoon, I was at a gymnasium in Paris, getting ready to finish the last hour of teaching. Over the weekend, I had been teaching 20 French students Wudang tai chi chuan. The mood was phenomenal; I was in the zone. But I also felt tired. It had been a long weekend, and I hadn't slept much over the last few days. This is also why I didn't put much stock in the fact that some of the students had trouble understanding my instructions. Several of them indicated that they couldn't hear or understand what I was saying. I could feel how I stumbled a bit over the words, but I figured it was probably just because I had been teaching in English all weekend.

But during the following dinner, it got worse, and I felt that I couldn't speak clearly at all. My tongue felt 20 times heavier than normal, and I had trouble using it when I talked. At the same time, my right eye had started acting strangely. Confused, I asked the guy next to me if he noticed anything different about my face. Astonished, he looked at me and said, "YES! You should go look at yourself in the mirror."

I got up quickly and went to the bathroom. I could see by his reaction that this wasn't good. When I got there, I could clearly see what he meant. There was something very wrong with the right side of my face. It wouldn't move a fraction of what it did before and seemed dull.

I told myself that it was probably just exhaustion and it would go away if I got some sleep. So, I went to bed early.

As I woke up the following day, I hurried to the bathroom and looked at myself in the mirror. Only to affirm that it had gotten a whole lot worse! All the right side of my face was paralyzed, and there was no life in it. At all. No matter what I did, it was just dead. *Alright, I need to go home NOW!* I thought and started getting a little scared.

When I finally got home, I just lay down in bed and stared at the ceiling. When my girlfriend came home and saw me, she was terrified. "You need to see the doctor, Torben! This is all wrong!" she said. And yes, she was right.

I went to the emergency room, where I was immediately hospitalized. But it took a while before a doctor could come around, so I just lay there waiting. I will never forget those hours I spent at the emergency room—in a room with others who had suffered things like strokes. I thought to myself, *What the heck is this? I'm not ill, so why am I here with people who are THAT ill?* That's when I suddenly came to think back on when my father was my age and he had suffered a stroke. They had discovered that he had blood cancer... *Shit, this isn't good, Torben,* I thought to myself.

As the doctor finally came, he was very serious and immediately started running several tests. They tested everything they could and took blood samples but came up with nothing. "We cannot find anything. So, there is only one thing to do, and that's to wait for the results from the blood samples. The results should be ready in a matter of days. Until then, we can do no more, so you are free to go home again. It will probably go away on its own before then," the doctor said.

"But, you must be able to do something or give me something to make this go away," I said. But there was nothing to do.

"Here. Try this," the nurse said, and gave me a training program for the facial muscles. "Do these exercises several times a day, in order for the facial nerves and the facial muscles to learn to react to the signals from the brain." It wasn't a miracle cure, but it was something that I could try.

Back in my living room, I now sat all alone on the couch and stared into the air. *What the heck is this? Why me? What had I done for this to happen to me?* I was completely knocked out and cancelled all of my appointments for the next few days. I did the exercises several times a day, but nothing happened. Every time I stood in front of a mirror, I looked for signs of improvement, but there were no signs at all.

I felt very much alone as I lay there on the couch, watching TV and staring out the window. I felt like an old man who couldn't take care of himself. Constantly drooling down my own stomach because I couldn't control it didn't make it any better. *If only the master could see me now!*

A week went by, and the blood samples hadn't given any explanation for my condition, so I was left to my own devices. There was no change in my face, and slowly it was dawning on me that I might have to live with this for the rest of my life.

The truth wanted to come out

For many years, I had the mindset that everything we meet on our way is there because there is something for us to learn. So the question was: what was I supposed to learn from this? For many hours a day, I lay there thinking about how my life had been. What challenges I had been through. Which people had really challenged and pushed me. What was it that I was supposed to learn?

I couldn't find the right answers and then started thinking about who might be able to help me. The name Christo Black came up. Christo had, many years ago, taught me healing. And even though I didn't practice it anymore, I was still in contact with him. So, I booked an appointment with him. A few days later, I was on my way there and was suddenly confident that he could help me.

We sat down, and I started telling him about the experiences of the past few years, and especially about the master's way of treating me. I could feel how everything turned inside me, and it felt as if I had a black cloud over my head. My whole body tensed up, and the anger, frustration, and rage welled up in me. Christo was listening patiently while nodding in recognition. I asked him several times if he felt that these experiences were outrageous, as well. Whether he could see how unfairly the master had treated me.

Just as I, in all my misery, was about to launch into the next story, he lifted his hand to signal that I was to stop talking. He got up and went to stand behind me. This completely confused me because I was in the middle of relaying all the important details that he no doubt needed in order to heal me from the bad treatment from others.

He put his hands on my shoulders and asked me to close my eyes. I did, even though it was hard for me. I felt like interrupting him because I felt he was progressing much too fast. But my respect for him made me close my eyes and shut up.

"Torben," he said, "how do you feel about losing face?"

Immediately, I opened my eyes and answered, "What do you mean?" I was just about to turn around and look at him, but he held me firmly in the chair. I felt tense and very upset. The fact that he held me in place didn't make things any better. My conclusion was that he had completely missed the point. I hadn't come to talk about myself, but to heal my...

"TORBEN!" he suddenly yelled.

This gave me a shock and interrupted my train of thought. He then squeezed my shoulders to signify his words: "Trust me." He then asked me to take a few deep breaths and close my eyes. Again. Shortly after, he asked me the same question: "How do you feel about losing face?"

Impatiently and slightly provoked, I answered: "But I feel fine about that!" Even though I deep down inside knew it was a lie.

And Christo knew it too. He asked again: "How do you feel about losing face? And this time you are not to answer before I say so. I want you to really consider this. I know you can."

I closed my eyes again and took a couple of deep breaths. After about 10 seconds, I already felt like giving the same answer again. Now I had thought plenty about it. But because he had taken that option from me, he had forced me to sit with it. And, annoyingly, as more time went by, the more I started relating to the question from another perspective. For some reason, I came to think of the mantra that I always happily shared with others: "Everything happens for a reason. There is something for you to learn." And that's how it was, just not with the master. It was pure and simple envy, and it had nothing to do with me. If anyone had something to learn, it was…

Suddenly Christo removed his hands from my shoulders. I opened my eyes and saw how he knelt down in front of me. His eyes were still closed as he placed one hand on my heart and the other on my stomach. I wasn't entirely sure what had happened, but it felt as if an explosion started inside my body. It felt as if the pain in my stomach intensified a thousand times, and at the same time I had a lump in my throat the size of a tennis ball.

I fought hard to keep it inside but felt my body going more and more out of control. Suddenly Christo opened his eyes and looked straight inside of me. "Torben, it is time you let go of your pride. It is time for you to free yourself. It is time for you to…let go."

His words hit the mark.

I completely crumpled. The tears were pouring out of me, as if they had waited a hundred years for this very moment. My entire body acknowledged the need for his words, and it felt as if it was the only medicine it hungered for. For every tear that fell, my body let go a little more. Not because of the tears but because I slowly realized what this was all about. Little by little, I understood what it was the master had tried to make me realize. He knew that I would never have listened to reason. He knew that my armor was too thick for him to penetrate with words. The only thing that would work was to let me realize that for myself.

Suddenly I understood what he had tried to teach me. In his very own unique way.

On my way home from Christo, it felt as if I wasn't even in this world. I was working hard to deal with all the new impressions that our meeting had started. It was as if a new programming was beginning inside me.

Something inside me had changed

In the following weeks, there was no change on my face. But that was okay. I was much more absorbed with reviewing the past many years in a new perspective.

One morning, I was brushing my teeth and noticed a microscopic movement from the right side of my nose. I came closer to the mirror and tried to repeat that movement. *Yes! It did it!* There was life in the nostril! In an almost miraculous fashion, my entire face started returning to its own self. And six months later, all was back to normal.

I never doubted for a second that as I had started understanding what the message was in all of my challenges, my body started reacting. The physical and mental pressure that I had carried for most of my life was gone, and my body suddenly felt freer than ever. I started to realize that many of the people I had met over the years, consciously or unconsciously, had tried to teach me to trust in myself, and not struggle to be better than other people.

It would take many years before I understood the message in the master's way of handling me. He had seen that I was controlled by my ego and that I was very focused on being recognized as one of his best students. Through one humiliation after another, he took apart my ego and the façade came apart little by little. I was just too proud to realize it.

I didn't react to his any attempts at teaching me in a kind way. That is why he ended up having to remove that which he knew was the most important to me. Which was my proof of being the best. I had to go through so much before finally catching on.

But now that I finally understood this, I could finally...**let go.**

A WARRIOR REBORN

For 20 years, I had a constant fear of making mistakes, afraid of not being the best. This all welled from the fear of losing love and respect. It manifested in an unending and insatiable need for recognition that guided my entire life. It was not until I let go that I felt how hard it was to live like that.

For many years, I had this inner feeling that I had a lot more to give. I could feel the master inside me, the true master who does not fight for his ego. I wished to let go of my ego and show my students the real Torben, but I feared if they came to know the truth about me, I would lose them. This is why I stayed in the "role" for many years.

I can hear myself sharing experiences over the years, influencing people around me to change, and it had been fantastic. A fantastic feeling to help others—but deep inside I fought a battle between the outer ego and the inner master.

Through the years, many students have asked me for advice, and I have given counsel by the best of my knowledge. I have been counseling and guiding and all the while I fought a battle to change my own life, but I was too proud to ask for advice—afraid that they would tell me what I already knew. That I should stop seeking the recognition of others. Let go of my ego and show myself as the one I am.

It took a harsh experience before I realized what really mattered. A wake-up call that came at just the right moment, as this kind of incident has a tendency to do. My face was paralyzed, and I experienced how the world just kept on going, business as usual, even though I lay there all alone. Everyone kept up their everyday lives, as though nothing had happened, while I lay there feeling sorry for myself. I had started letting the poison spread through my body.

> *One does not die from snakebite—the bite on its own doesn't kill. It's the poison that courses through your body afterwards that is the killer. And this you can do something about, if you don't just lie down and feel sorry for yourself.*

We often hear stories about people who have changed their lives after traumatic experiences. But we don't have to wait for a traumatic experience. We always have a choice. But that demands of us that we become aware of where we are, what we feel, where we want to go, and what our next move should be.

Most importantly, we have to understand what it is that has been keeping us back for so many years. What we have been using as an excuse for not doing it earlier. We have to understand that letting go doesn't mean to give up. On the contrary, it actually means that we are taking responsibility for our choices up until today. Then we can take full responsibility for our future development.

Letting go is about taking responsibility. About finding an understanding of what happened in the past and accepting that what has happened is in the past. It is about taking full responsibility for our feelings about the meanings of the things we have been through and knowing that as we change the way in which we see the world, the world we look upon will change.

I look back at the way my father brought me up and thank him with all my heart. *Thank you for encouraging me to do my best. Thank you for trying to teach me to be independent of others' opinions about me and what I do. I take responsibility for taking so long to learn the last part.*

The same goes for my master through 25 years. *Thank you for your patience through the years, and thank you for your persistence; you kept on, even though I didn't understand that message right away. The message was that it's not about being better than everyone else but about being better than who I was yesterday. That it's about development and being independent of the opinions of others, even those of my own master.*

From being SOMEONE to BEING

After I let go and took responsibility for my actions and interpretations of the past, changes within soon came— everything from a greater self-confidence to an excess energy for handling life and less concern about what others thought.

But the absolute greatest difference was the peace within me. The freedom to be the one that I deeply felt I really was without having to worry about what others thought or felt about me. In my everyday life it gave me freedom to just be myself, without having to perform to gain recognition. I just had to be myself. I rested within myself like never before, and I allowed myself not to be perfect. I was faithful to my heart and myself.

I took a while and lots of practice, but it paid off in the end. Today I have none of the insecurity I felt earlier in life. I dare to stand by my opinions and am less worried about what others might think. By letting go of the fear of losing others' love or admiration, I have found the peace in being myself and appreciate those who have chosen to spend time with me on a daily basis.

It may sound as if I don't care, but that is hardly the case. It is more a confidence in that everything is as it should be and when I am being true to myself and I present myself as who I am, then I attract people who complement where I am now.

I also know that nothing lasts forever, so I let go and feel grateful for the love that surrounds me. I am thankful for my strong body and my good health. I know that everything changes, but I let go and feel grateful.

I used to train to become better than everyone else, to impress everyone else—not only by winning the gold medals, but also by being able to tell others how much I trained. It is different today, after having let go of seeking the recognition of others. Today I am training for my own sake, not in order to impress others, but in order to tend to and strengthen my body physically and mentally. I train because I cannot help it. It is a part of me. I train as much as before, some days more than others, but I am motivated by something completely different, and that gives me peace and freedom. I have the choice and choose what is best for me.

My own role as master

I clearly remember how I used to feel personally attacked every time a student criticized me or my way of teaching. I was ready to fight. I reacted this way because criticism equaled failure to me. That is why I defended myself the best I had learned and tried to find an explanation that justified my actions. Even when I knew that they were right.

But this didn't make a particularly good master. I was always vulnerable to the opinions of my students, and that's why I unconsciously tried to satisfy them, so they wouldn't criticize me.

A quote from my teacher's book *Complete Tai Chi Chuan*, sums up how I was lacking as a master:

"Do not become one of these armchair experts. There are so many talking about it, but when it comes down to it, they themselves are unable to do it. Do not be one of those, but listen to your body, follow your heart, and decide to be true to yourself by going all the way."

I was becoming an expert on tai chi chuan but realized that part of me was becoming an armchair expert: a person who speaks a lot about what is mentally possible but has trouble actually going through it himself; a person who instructs others about the right strategies but has not successfully utilized them yet.

When I, for instance, heard myself saying: "The warrior must do what is right, let go, and be true to himself," I knew, that it wasn't something that I mastered for myself yet. I couldn't physically feel it when I said it out loud.

But after I let go, on that day, something happened. When my students gave me feedback, asked questions, or criticized me directly, I didn't feel insulted. This meant that I could view the things being said much more objectively and deal with it with a much more open attitude.

Often the exclamations from the students came as a result of them feeling frustrated, stressed, disappointed in themselves, or just having lost their way. Some students were just having a bad day. And when we reach that point, the easiest thing is to reject responsibility and throw blame at others. It is normal. But the big difference was that I didn't take it personally anymore. And even if it was directed at me, I no longer got defensive like I used to. Instead, I felt a calling to listen and be open to either suggestions or to pull the student from their own limiting thoughts and reestablish their faith in themselves—as a true master would. I was on my way.

Now I am focused on teaching the students at their own level; the ultimate goal is to raise the student, not promote myself.

As I feel more present, I notice my students much more. I sense when someone needs a little more attention. I never would have been able to do this if I hadn't let go and become more attentive.

My teaching became complete

I was beginning to feel that I had less and less focus on myself and more on what the students needed in the moment. As I wasn't concerned about gaining their recognition, I could be more attentive and read the students far better. More and more often I realized how the students' own egos prevented them from enjoying the training. I knew all the signals from myself. This is why I, very quickly, could adjust my teaching and communication to the individual student, to let them achieve the optimal from the classes. I had become more aware that the students didn't "just" come to be taught in tai chi chuan, that it was much more than that. I myself had learned so much more than tai chi chuan from my teacher, so I understood that my task was greater as such. I had become more conscious about doing what I talked about and so had become one who showed the way and not just talked about it.

My teaching had become more complete because it wasn't just movements I taught. It was a philosophy of life. I had become aware that my way in this world had taken a brand new turn, which was so different to how I started so many years ago. Then it had been to learn the martial art, to be able to toss around others, to become the best. Today my goal is to help others find their way through tai chi chuan and the entire life philosophy behind it.

This doesn't mean that my teachings are perfect, but that they are complete. They contain everything—we have a focus on the human being as a whole and not just the physical art of movement. Several times I have heard students say that my teaching has changed over the years, and to the positive. They cannot put words to it, but I believe that what they mean is that I have changed.

I am proud that today I am a better role model to my children, students, and others. When I speak of living by the old Taoist life philosophy, I have a happy feeling in my body because I know that I do my absolute best to live by the philosophy I speak of. I am not perfect, but I am very much aware about being true to myself and follow my heart. No matter the opinion of others.

Let Go
of What?

THE 3 STEPS TO LETTING GO

You've heard a lot about my journey and how I learned, the hard way, to let go. It was hard because I didn't know what I was looking for. I felt the symptoms, but I didn't understand their significance, and even more importantly, I didn't know what to do about them.

Luckily the symptoms are relatively easy to spot because they are often a large part of your life. And the better we become at recognizing them, the easier it will eventually become to let go.

Once we have realized that there is something we need to let go of, there is some preparation for us to do before we can be free. We cannot just jump ahead and potentially create a new situation just as bad as the old one. We need to establish a reason for why we have done as we have for all these years. We need to establish what we should learn from those experiences. And we need to figure out our own part in it all. And most importantly, we need to let go.

Through the following pages I will present to you the process that I guide my students through. It consists of three steps that the tai chi master uses when he wishes to create changes in his life. Make sure to take your time for each step, do the exercises, and go through them several times before moving on.

STEP 1: THE INVISIBLE CAUSE

Everything we have met and been through has helped to make us who we are today. No matter what we have experienced, we have added some meaning to it, which we take with us through life. Our experiences have taught us to develop certain skills to use in everyday situations. Among them, we have learned how to act, how we should be, and what we cannot do or cannot be.

Luckily, most of our experiences have had positive effects on us. They improve the way in which we see and use ourselves. As you might expect, these are not the ones we are going to discuss here. No, those we need to find are those that have had negative influences on us. Those that unconsciously have an influence on our thoughts, decisions, and actions.

Here I will start by sharing some of the most popular symptoms of holding on to negativity and experiences that might have caused them:

1. When we try to hide something

An example of this is when we "forget" to tell the whole truth about an experience and leave out the parts that we're not proud of. When we say that we run 10 kilometers a day, but the truth is that we haven't been running for months. When we say we make a lot of money but really have difficulties meeting ends.

What is the hidden reason? Where does it come from?

The reason could lie within our low self-esteem and that we have a need to raise ourselves up in order to get the recognition of others. At some point we learned that we weren't good enough. We learned that we had to perform in order to be anyone.

This most likely comes from those authority figures we have had through our lives—parents, teachers, other relatives, etc. We have adopted their points of view and given them too much value throughout our lives. Throughout our lives we have confirmed those points of view by letting them dictate how we behave.

2. When we deny responsibility

When we use sentences like these, we are typically denying responsibility: "I am as I am;" "I grew up in an orphanage;" "My parents are dead;" "I am an only child;" "I am the oldest;" "I am the youngest;" "I grew up in the countryside;" "I grew up in the city;" "I grew up in a poor family;" or "I grew up in a rich family."

What is the hidden reason? Where does it come from?

The reason could be that, as children, something or someone else got blamed when we got hurt. "It was that stupid door." "Oh, poor you! Stupid door!" We might have had overprotective parents that always dealt with our challenges for us.

It could come from experiences that were actually our own fault. But we managed, with success, to put the blame onto someone else. And since we were successful once, it most likely wasn't the last time, even if we felt bad deep down inside. If we could get away with it by lying, we learned that we didn't have to take responsibility.

3. When we encounter resistance

Sometimes we encounter resistance from others and deflect rather than being true to ourselves. Resistance can also come from within: "I probably can't do that anyway;" "I am not good enough;" "I can't figure this out;" and so on. Resistance from without can come in shape of the doubters, who themselves are struggling with their lives.

What is the hidden reason? And where does it come from?

The reason could be that we become insecure when others question what we say or do. When we encounter resistance, we think that we're probably the ones mistaken. The others are probably right. They know better.

This might originate from us not having learned to stand firm. We haven't practiced this skill. We may have been working on an assignment that we couldn't solve and then have gotten used to our parents solving it for us. We got the solution, but not the skill to solve the problem. We didn't get to learn to meet the resistance with curiosity and patience.

4. When we are judgmental

When we judge others, we remove focus from ourselves and point at them. For instance, we judge others in traffic who are speeding—without knowing who they are or what is going on in their lives. We judge the homeless, the obese, the skinny, etc.

What is the hidden reason? Where does it come from?

The reason is that by judging others we remove responsibility from ourselves and that with which we struggle. I am pretty sure that we have all done something in traffic that wasn't all that smart. But we keep that to ourselves while we point at others. We learn by observing others, and if our closest role models point at others, well, then we learn from that.

This stems from the fact that we, in our society, have learned what is "normal"; we have learned that if you stick out from the crowd, you're wrong. We have learned how we ought to behave, and if someone's different, we are quick to judge. Otherwise, we would be the ones who are "wrong." This is very obvious in school, where the students can be very hard on one another.

5. When we speak of and focus on the negative

When we bring focus to the negative in our lives, we remove focus from everything we could actually achieve. When our focus is on our shortcomings and that which we cannot do, it gives us an excuse not to do anything about it. When we focus on our shortcomings, we, for instance, don't need to practice nearly as much as we actually should.

What is the hidden reason? Where does it come from?

The reason is often that it is safe to focus on that which isn't possible. Then we're not disappointing others or ourselves. This gives us a pass to slide on through our lives without achieving any of those things we really dream of. At the same time, if we are negative, we make others give us positive attention, and that is better than no attention at all.

This may come from what we have seen and learned over the years. We may have seen people close to us get a lot of attention because they were ill, and we, not being ill, didn't get nearly the same attention. When learned that those who were sick and negative got more care and attention.

6. When we suppress our feelings

Even when we suppress our feelings and sweep them under the carpet, they will often be lurking in the background. Several small things will make them accumulate, and someday, when we are under pressure, they will all come out in an uncontrolled explosion.

What is the hidden reason? Where does it come from?

The reason often is that we do not handle the matter at hand while the feeling is present. It may look insignificant on the surface, and we would like to avoid any possible conflict. The paradox is that exactly this will only lead to an even greater conflict the day the cup is full and we react inappropriately.

This may come from not having learned to talk things over as we grew up. Actually, we do not need to go very far back in time to discover that it was very normal NOT to talk about such things. Just like it was not normal to express our problems.

7. When we are too protective

When we are too protective, it is often the fear that surfaces, fearing an accident would happen. One example could be our roles as parents: We want the very best for our children, and some parents go as far as to being constantly vigilant and overprotective of their children. They constantly see disaster happening and are afraid that their children will be hurt.

What is the hidden reason? Where does it come from?

The reason is that we wish to protect our children, which is quite natural. But the opposite might happen, as they never learn to deal with the various situations themselves. This also gives us a feeling of significance, that our children need us and we are important. It is very important to us that there is a meaning to life, and protecting our children is one. This may come from having experienced this in our own upbringing. It might also be that we have lost someone in an accident, and thus will do anything to make sure this doesn't happen to our child. Our instinct is to look after our children. The dangers in the world around us are actually quite limited, but our instincts are still there.

8. When we are afraid

When we are afraid to fail, we become insecure and don't dare to take action. We know what we should do, but we are afraid to do it. What if we fail? Or what if it's wrong? We are afraid of not being good enough to be loved. When we are afraid, and the fear of failure is dimming everything, we hold back. We are afraid to show others who we really are. We are limiting ourselves.

What is the hidden reason? Where does it come from?

The reason is that we have a deeply rooted need to feel loved. And when love is at stake, the fears come forth. We forget to listen to ourselves and follow the current. We may have experienced others in our lives who have lived their entire lives in the shadows of their partners. A life in which that person always talked about all the dreams she had but was afraid to chase them. Out of fear of losing her partner.

This may come from having heard these sentences so many times that in the end we start believing them: "If you do that, I will leave you!" or "If you do that, you can count me out!" When you have one threat after another thrown at you, you learn to be afraid of the consequences of your decisions, which will make you hesitate in the future.

Exercise

"How do I find the hidden reason?"

This you do by paying attention to how you react. Think back and look at how you react under pressure. How you handle criticism. Whether you are quick in judging others. Whether you give in when faced with resistance, and so on.

Decide over a period of one week to finish every day by going through and answering the questions on the next page.

Today I caught myself hiding from...
"I did so because I was afraid of..."
"I believe it comes from..."

Today I didn't take responsibility for...
"I did so because I was afraid of ..."
"I believe it comes from..."

Today I caught myself taking the role of the victim when...
"I did so because I was afraid of..."
"I believe it comes from..."

Today I caught myself giving up when I encountered resistance in the form of...
"I did so because I was afraid of..."
"I believe it comes from..."

Today I caught myself being judgmental when...
"I did so because I was afraid of..."
"I believe it comes from..."

Today I caught myself reacting negatively when...said...
"I did so because I was afraid of..."
"I believe it comes from..."

Today I felt a fear of...
"I did so because I was afraid of..."
"I believe it comes from..."

Today I caught myself bending the truth when...
"I did so because I was afraid of..."
"I believe it comes from..."

STEP 2: THE LESSON UNDERNEATH

My master humiliated me. He relentlessly picked on me and pointed out my flaws. I was 100 percent certain he didn't like me at all. But the truth was that he was trying to teach me something. He had tried being kind, but I was addicted to the positive attention. And that was one of the reasons why I reacted so intensely. Because he challenged an addiction of mine! A limiting and unhealthy part of my personality that he had to help me get rid of.

As I stood there in front of the mirror, with one half of my face paralyzed, it was very hard to see the deeper meaning in everything. It is always like this as things are occurring. But I believe that there will always be a meaning and that there is something for us to learn. Provided we want to.

There are hidden messages in everything we experience and in all the people we meet. And yes, here I mean everyone without exception. Whether it is our parents, siblings, extended family, good friends or acquaintances, colleagues, neighbors, etc.

Nothing is accidental, and life is so clearly designed that we have an opportunity to learn from every experience and especially from our mistakes. Wherever we have failed, reacted inappropriately, or become ashamed just by thinking back on what we did when we came under pressure, we need to use these experiences constructively, learn from them, and use our wisdom to create the life we dream of.

The challenge is to spot these gifts. It demands of us that we pay more attention to our earlier experiences and reflect upon what we could learn from these past experiences and the people associated with them, no matter what we have been through. This can be difficult. If, for instance, we keep justifying to ourselves that the "blame" lies with others, then we will never see the gift.

Instead we will hang on to the specific experience and only focus on what that experience did to us in that moment. We feel sorry for ourselves. Blame others for not being able to shake off this experience. We focus on what others did instead of focusing on the value and meaning that we put into the experience afterwards. We become a victim.

As long as we do nothing about it, life will keep sending new challenges our way. Experiences that will give us new possibilities to learn that which we refused to learn last time. Each time it happens, more and more emotional pressure will be put on us; each time we refuse to learn the lesson, the sacrifice will become even larger. It is much easier for us to see what others need to do in order to improve their lives. But often, when it concerns ourselves, we choose not to see it.

Those standing beside us can often clearly see that we (the victims) are going in the wrong direction and that we cling to our roles because it's what's easiest for us to do. It is clear to them that we do not want to admit our responsibility and then choose the easiest immediate solution. We do not see that things will only get worse and worse, and should they feel like confronting us with it, we immediately defend ourselves! "You do not understand! It's not the same! You don't know how hard it is! I cannot just change!"

This is why it is essential that we practice our ability to reflect more than to judge. We should also be better at seeing our own part in the experiences we are exposed to and understand that it's essentially something we have "ordered." They are the teachers who are there to help us grow. When we finally realize what we were supposed to learn, we can take this lesson with us and create the life we've dreamt of.

How do we figure out what we were supposed to learn? Essentially we can divide any experience into 3 steps that will help us view it from a healthier perspective:

1. What was it this person wanted to teach me?

2. What did I learn?

3. What was the deeper meaning?

1. What was it this person wanted to teach me?

The first step is to try to look at the experience from a new perspective—namely that the person basically had good intentions, even though it may not have appeared that way.

We need to see this person as a "teacher" and try to look behind their actions. What was it that they wanted to teach us? What was their intention?

2. What did I learn?

Once we have found something that makes sense, we must focus on what we actually chose to learn from it. How we interpreted the experience. Which qualities or convictions we developed and brought with us through life.

3. What was the lesson underneath?

And as we have focused on the point or profit of this singular experience, we have to look at it from an even greater perspective. As we are repeatedly exposed to the same or similar challenges, what is it that the universe wants to teach us? Is there a deeper meaning?

EXAMPLE:
A girl had been diagnosed with diabetes at age two. She was marked as "ill" by the ones closest to her and had been completely overprotected throughout her upbringing. In her 40s, she recalled that she had experienced illness for as long as she could remember. She was very angry with her mother because she had always been fussing over her. There was no doubt that it was her mother's fault that she didn't feel she had any energy to pursue her dreams.

One afternoon, she was sitting across from me, frustrated, with tears in her eyes, and said that she was so tired of being treated as though she was ill. Instead of asking further about that, I just asked her this: "What if we play with the thought that your mother always had the best of intentions. Then what would you think she tried to teach you?"

She sat there in silence and wondered about that. Then, after some hesitation, it came to her: "I believe that she just wanted to protect me from the world. And teach me, that I have to take extra good care of myself, being as ill as I am."

"Okay, does that make sense to you?" I asked her.

"Yes, it actually does," she replied while reflecting on it.

"Fine. I wish to ask you something else then. What did you learn from this treatment that you received from your mother? How did this upbringing affect you through your life?"

All was quiet as she sat for a long time and contemplated her life with diabetes and all the other things she had experienced. "I learned that I was never as good as everyone else, that I could never do the same as everyone else. That people should always take extra precautions around me in order to protect me from all the dangers in the world."

I looked at her and asked again, "Okay, does that make sense to you?"

She nodded.

"Okay. In conclusion, I want you to answer this: what you believe the deeper meaning was with all that you have been through?"

She sat for a long time contemplating this and finally answered, "I actually believe, that my mother wanted to teach me to stand up for myself!" Tears were running down her cheeks. "Throughout my entire life I have been a pleaser. Someone who always made sure that others felt good and always did what others saw as right. Exactly like my mother! And I have hated it! And the more my mother told me what to do, the angrier I got with her. But I never said so…"

"Torben, this makes complete sense," she said with a huge smile covering her face. "Throughout my life I have tried to prove to everyone else that I can do what I want. And when they told me that someone in my condition shouldn't, it just made me want to prove it to them. But I never told them that I didn't want their advice. Instead I just did the opposite of what they told me."

"Fantastic," I said. "Then perhaps the time has come to tell them that you do not wish for their well-intended advice anymore? And perhaps it is time for you to stop doing things in spite, instead of from want? And perhaps even apologize to your mother, inside, for hating her when she actually wanted to teach you something?"

She looked at me with wet eyes and quietly said, "Thank you…"

1. What was it they wanted to teach her?

They wanted to teach her that life is full of limitations. And that she—with her illness—should be aware that she was not like all the other children. That she always had to take care not to get hurt.

2. What did she learn?

She learned that she wasn't like everyone else. That she was "weak." So weak that she couldn't do all the things other children did. She learned that she wasn't good enough, that she was flawed. In time it developed into a need to disprove and fight to get rid of the opinions of others.

3. What was the lesson underneath?

She had to find confidence in herself to not let herself be guided by the opinions of others. She needed to set boundaries and tell people that she didn't need their advice.

The comprehension of what had happened and why it happened frees us. A freedom beyond comparison. And once we understand the significance of other peoples' "parts," it becomes much easier to contain them. Then we will stop hating them and start to appreciate them.

There will always be people, both known and unknown, who are trying to teach us something. Testing our boundaries. Our integrity. Our values. They are there to make us better. And even though we see it as if they, consciously or unconsciously, are trying to pull us down, there is a deeper gift for us.

EXAMPLE:

Birgit: *I'm self-employed and have difficulty getting things done. It is a major problem because there is only me to do it. I am just not particularly disciplined. Actually, I hate everything that resembles discipline. It makes me itch!*

Torben: *Okay, so what you're saying is that you lack discipline?*

She looked at me with acknowledgment.

Torben: *Let us take a look at what it is about the word discipline; from where does your resentment come from?*

Birgit: *It definitely comes from my childhood, where my father was very disciplinary. I had to do everything properly, in his way, in his tempo, and make sure that everything was perfect.*

Torben: *Okay, so it would be fair to say that he was something of a perfectionist?*

Birgit: *Yes! Nothing was ever good enough. And that is how I feel today!*

She looked at me with a crooked smile.

Torben: *Are you aware what the word perfectionist is equal to?*

Birgit: *No, I don't know.*

Torben: It is equal to fear and insecurity. The fear of failing and a constant uncertainty of whether what you do is good enough.

Birgit: That seems to fit quite well with me, but what does that have to do with my feelings about the word discipline?

Torben: You hate the word discipline because you connect it to everything your father told you to do. So when you hear the word discipline, all your old emotions and experiences well back up again. Correct?

Birgit: Yes, that is right...

Torben: So what if I told you that it isn't your father who's in charge anymore? And that you can do exactly as you please, any which way it pleases you. For instance, you could create the business you dream of, in the way you feel like, but it still demands discipline. The difference is that this time it is you who decides what needs to be done, at what pace and how.

Let us take a look back at what it was that your father wanted to teach you. What do you think it was?

Birgit: He wanted to teach me to do things perfectly. I might as well just do it properly from the start, or I would have to do it over.

Torben: Okay, and what did you learn from that upbringing? What did you bring along in terms of *thoughts and habits that have prevented you from living the life you feel you are capable of?*

Birgit: *I learned that nothing was ever good enough. That everything had to be perfect before I felt good enough. I learned that mistakes were bad and that I would never live up to my father's expectations.*

Torben: *So this is what you chose to learn. If we look more generally at this, then what do you believe is the deeper meaning with you having to go through all this? What did the universe try to teach you?*

Birgit: *I am pretty sure that I was to learn to say no, to be independent of other people's opinions about me and what I do. I also believe that I was to learn that mistakes are not bad, but a step closer to the goal.*

Torben: *So this actually means that you need to treat yourself better. Not set the standards so high that they become impossible to achieve. The most important part is that you get started. You have to do things because you feel that it is the right thing to do and not to prove anything to your father or anyone else.*

Birgit: *Oh, you are so right! I can feel that you are right!*

Torben: *So how do you feel now when I say that it takes discipline to achieve what you want?*

Birgit: *I feel fantastic about that! I have always been able to be disciplined; I have just never felt like it. But* *now it has a completely different meaning, and I feel more like using it!*

1. What was it they wanted to teach her?

They wanted to teach her to do things properly from the start. That discipline is the most important. That she needs to be a perfectionist to achieve anything. And if she's not, she will never succeed.

2. What did she learn?

She learned that she had to be a perfectionist, that nothing was ever good enough. She learned that discipline is equal to pain, boredom, and pressure and that there was no room for doing things her own way.

3. What was the lesson underneath?

It was that everything is perfect the way it is and that perfectionists are filled with fear and insecurity and a fear of failure—a feeling of uncertainty about what they are doing being good enough. She had to learn that discipline is actually a good thing, as long she sets the agenda. She needed to let go of her father's prejudices, find confidence in herself, and be disciplined—for her own sake.

EXERCISE

"How do I spot the lesson underneath?"

To find the lesson underneath, you must now take one of your experiences from the previous exercise and then ask yourself the three questions.

It can be hard to begin with, especially if it is something recent. That is why it may be a good idea to choose something that you are not emotionally influenced by right now. After all, you are just learning this skill, so start with a minor challenge and practice your skill at going deeper with your experiences from the past.

Complete these sentences:

1. That which they/he/she wanted to teach me was that I had to...

2. That which I learned through this experience was that through life I have…

3. The deeper meaning with meeting these people and the purpose of this experience was that...
"I believe it is because..."

STEP 3: MAKE PEACE AND LET GO

Okay, so far so good. Now you know how to spot the invisible cause and what lesson it taught you. Before we can entirely let go, it is important that we acknowledge that we ourselves have chosen where we are. Our lives are reflections of the choices we have made, and that may be one of the hardest acknowledgments for many of us. It would imply that we have a responsibility for being where we are—no matter where that is and what has happened.

Once we acknowledge and take responsibility for our actions in the past, we are simultaneously saying that we take full responsibility for what we do from here and on. It may be scary, because it means that we no longer have any excuses to hold us back. On the other hand, it is one of the most liberating things.

Once we take responsibility of how we have handled our experiences from the past, we set ourselves free to move freely in the future. It may be overstepping some boundaries, but the heavy backpack is suddenly lighter, and we can move more freely, with daily practice.

They did their best.

I choose to believe that we always do the best we can from what we have learned and the given situation we are currently in. Could we have done better at another time? Probably. But in this instance, we do the best we can. The same goes for every other person around us—including our parents.

I believe that all parents wish the very best for their children. And they will do the very best they can, with their basis being what they have learned. But, like us, they also have their inner struggles with the past, which means that sometimes they do not react as well as they could. If, for instance, they knew what you now know.

Luckily many of our parents themselves are pattern breakers.

They may have experienced violence in their childhood and have nobly chosen another path as they became parents.

They chose a path based on their experiences. Some of what they got from their parents they brought along, and other things they separated from. They did their very best, and even if we might not always think that is the case, then the time might have come to acknowledge their attempts, forgive them, accept it, and let go.

Not for their sake, but for your own.

Jacob: From when I was 15 to when I was 17, parties, hash, and drinking were the only things I cared about. And even if that sounds pretty normal, with me it was extreme. I didn't care at all about anything or anyone, and it was very hard on my family. It soon became an addiction that I couldn't escape. Today I am really embarrassed about it because I can really see how poorly I treated people close to me.

Torben: Did you have fun back then?

Jacob: Yes, of course. I was constantly stoned and walked around in my own little world. But now that it is over, I cannot help but think about what I put my parents and siblings through.

Torben: How often do you think about it?

Jacob: Almost daily. It's been six years since I got out of it, so it is in the past, and I feel good today.

Torben: That is not exactly what I hear you saying. You say that you feel good today, but at the same time you're saying that you're embarrassed about what you did to your family back then. Have you taken responsibility for your actions, acknowledged your responsibility in it all, and told this to your family?

Jacob: I have apologized, but I felt bad because of things at school, so I started hanging out with some shady characters, and they got me into the substance abuse…

Torben: So what is your responsibility in this, Jacob?

Jacob: I am just thinking that there are circumstances that drove me into it… Otherwise I wouldn't have done it.

Torben: I completely understand that you didn't feel good at school and that you may have had some challenges at home. But who made the decision about hanging out with those shady characters?

Jacob: I did.

Torben: Okay. Who made the decision about smoking hash?

Jacob: I did.

Torben: And who made the decision about drinking?

Jacob: I did.

Torben: Who made the decision to let your family suffer for it?

Jacob: I did…

Tears began welling in Jacob's eyes.

Torben: So we agree that it was your responsibility that you smoked hash, drank, and were stoned all the time?

Jacob: Yes.

Torben: Okay, so since you're still embarrassed about it, which is okay, I think it is about time that you acknowledge your responsibility. I want you to get ahold of all your family and tell them so.

Jacob looked at me, scared.

Torben: Yes, I am serious about this. I really recommend you acknowledge your responsibility and the fact that your decisions affected the whole family for years. I completely understand that you needed help, but right now it is about you taking responsibility. Your family deserves a sincere apology, and you deserve to let go of your bad conscience and all the blame that you are always hitting yourself over the head with.

Jacob: Yes, you are right. They deserve a sincere apology, and I am ready to take full responsibility for my actions. I deserve to let the past go.

A few weeks later, we again sat facing each other. This time he was an entirely different man, a grown man, sitting with a straight back and looking proud.

Torben: How do you feel?

Jacob: I feel fantastic! I have never felt as free as I do today. I got ahold of my entire family and told them that I was sorry about everything. And I acknowledged that it was my responsibility and my decisions that had led to my substance abuse. The whole family accepted my apology and praised me for taking responsibility. They said that they would *support me no matter which way I might choose in the future and were happy that I had gotten this far in relation to where I once was. They actually said that they were proud of me…*

Jacob had tears in his eyes.

The art of forgiving one's self

When I asked Jacob to contact his family, acknowledge his responsibility, and apologize, it was as much for his sake as for his family. He had carried that guilt for several years and blamed himself every day for all the pain and grief he had given them. It was about time that he let go, and in order to do so, he had to face his fear, acknowledge his responsibility, and give his whole family a sincere apology. Only in this way could he let go and set himself free.

The same applies to the rest of us if we carry around guilt and shame.

For a long time after my own insight, I blamed myself for not having recognized this sooner. I hated myself for my thoughts of my master and the things I had said. Only when I forgave myself and accepted that I had done my best was it possible to free myself.

I had to accept that my actions reflected the condition I was under at the time. I acknowledged that I had many chances to learn the lesson, but for some reason I wasn't ready. I did the best I could.

Below, you can follow how my process of acknowledgement looked:

I accept and acknowledge that it was my responsibility, what I did about the experience I had as a child. It was my responsibility to change my view of the experience and change the way in which I made my choices following that experience—the choice was mine and mine alone.

I acknowledge that I blamed my father for not living as the one I deep inside felt that I was. I accept that it was my choice and that in the future I have the power to choose another path.

I acknowledge that no matter what trials I have been through, what resistance and challenges I have faced, that how much value I gave these experiences has always been my choice. I have always had the choice to choose another path than the one I did.

I acknowledge that I have been focused on achieving the recognition of others and that it was completely and entirely my choice to strive for their acceptance of my projects and me. I know that I, at any given time, had the choice and the opportunity to change it but didn't and that it was my responsibility. I have the power and the opportunity to do so now.

I acknowledge that I feared losing my girlfriend, so I did just what she expected of me. I wasn't myself, and it was my choice, and the result was that she left me…

EXERCISE

"How do I make peace and become free?"

In order to truly let go, we need to accept that things are in the past. No matter what has happened, it is done and cannot be changed. We must accept and acknowledge that it was our responsibility, the weight we gave the experience, and the convictions that follow.

This also demands that we forgive those who were involved, no matter what they contributed. It is not for their sake, but for ours. We must release them and the past in order to let go. We must forgive ourselves for living with this conviction through our lives. We must forgive ourselves for not doing something about this earlier.

Acceptance, acknowledgement, and forgiveness are the keys to finally letting go.

Complete these sentences:

1. I accept that they did it because that was what they had learned. I realize/acknowledge that I have blamed them for not living the life I knew deep down that I could because...

2. I acknowledge that the value of the experience, the weight of it, and the consequences that the convictions following have had on my life are my responsibility and mine alone. I accept that I have been hanging on to them because...

3. I forgive _____ and accept that _____ did the best he/she could at that given time under those circumstances.

4. I admit that it was my own responsibility that I...

5. I acknowledge, take responsibility for, and forgive myself for not doing something about this sooner. I know that it is in the past and that I can go wherever I want as long as I acknowledge that I have always had a choice.

Let Go
WITHOUT
GIVING UP

WHAT DOES IT TAKE?

The quest for gold and glory has been my greatest motivation for many, many years, and through this I have achieved many, many results and many, many things. But it has also been a life in which the fear of failing has been dominant.

I have always trained a lot, mostly in order to be in great shape. But I was driven by being better, faster, and stronger than anyone else. I fought my way through by discipline and determination. I have always been focused on the next competition, the next harvest of medals, and the next event at which I could gain recognition.

Nowadays, when I rise in the morning, the day looks entirely different. As my alarm goes off, I start my day by saying: "It's going to be a good day, a great day, and I look forward to it." Afterwards, I take a deep breath and hold it for a while as I create the feeling of a fantastic day in my entire body. I drink my morning shake and get ready for my one-and-a-half-hour nei kung morning workout.

There is no pressure today. I do it for my own sake. I have no intention of impressing anybody, winning gold, or getting mentioned in the local newspaper. I do it solely because I want to be the most optimal version of myself and because I want to have a fantastic life with my children and future grandchildren. I will show my children the way instead of talking about it.

Many believe that it is only special people with unique talents that have the necessary drive to be good at something. But the truth is that we all practice harder and even longer than the so-called "World's Best." Often we just don't realize that we are actually doing it. And what's worse is that even though we practice so intensely, it isn't necessarily the best for us.

Take myself, for instance. For more than 20 years I focused daily on how I could prove to others that I was the best. Everything from my way of training to the way I walk. Every time I met someone new, I was dedicated to convincing this person of my worth. All I was focused on was convincing the rest of the world that I was good enough. I was dedicated, focused, and persistent…without being conscious about it. Every day—from I rose in the morning until I went to bed—I practiced this characteristic and became very good at it. Even though I was further and further demolishing my true self…

What we need to do is to use the skills we already possess in order to create the life we dream of. All we need to do is to take the toothbrush into the other hand if we wish to be better at brushing our teeth with the other hand. The hand we already use is a world champion at brushing teeth. We have trained it for so many years that we know the method. Now we simply have to start training the other hand. It really is that simple.

And yet the fewest among us would start brushing our teeth with the opposite hand unless we had a broken arm. We know that it is simple to think positively, and we know that it works, but yet we do not practice it consciously. Fact is that no matter how simple it may sound, we need to practice it many times before it feels natural.

We have all practiced for many years!

Imagine carrying around various convictions like: *"I am not good enough;" "I am too fat;" "I will never succeed;" "I will never be as good as the others;"* or *"I will never find a sweetheart."* Then there is a great chance that you—every single day—are repeating this in your head. And for every time you have a thought that supports your conviction, you grow this muscle bigger. As you may figure out, it doesn't take much before you grow strong in your negative convictions.

Once we finally decide to aim higher and quit thinking that way, we often do so without thinking it through properly. We have no plan for how to do it. We have no plan for how to let go of the bad habits. Instead we just "try" to implement new ones. And it doesn't take much time before it becomes difficult. And as soon as we start sweating the slightest, we decide that we're doing okay anyway.

We have learned that if we're ill, then we go to the doctor and expect him to fix us. Which he usually does with either a scalpel or pills. Then we feel alright again and keep going. We have learned to have other people fix us when we need repairs. It just doesn't work when we want to change old habits that we have practiced for many years. Unfortunately, there is no pill for that.

It absolutely isn't easy to change your habits, but it isn't that hard either. The problem often is that we start out too big. We start with goals that are much too large and break our necks going there because the task soon feels enormous. Our expectations about handling our problems in a hurry are much too big. We deceive ourselves into thinking that it can't be that hard. And then we feel like a failure when we haven't—three days later—solved the problem.

Changing our habits looks easy and sounds so simple, but it takes many hours of practice over time. It's the simple things that get things going. It's the little things that create results. Then what we need to bring out is the acknowledgement that this is going to take a while and that is all right. We need to have patience and focus on the simple things in our everyday lives that will make the big difference.

If you're running a marathon, you do not consider how many kilometers you have left. You consider the next step and the next step. It is all the many single steps that get you through a marathon. When it comes to letting go and finding that inner ultimate power, we need to focus on the simple things. Simple things in our everyday lives that will, over time, make the big difference. We need to focus more on how we appear in any given situation, than on how quickly we develop.

You will find that the exercises I will ask you to do are both simple and easy. But if you take them too lightly or advance too quickly to the next step, you will fall right into the trap. Here it is about acknowledging and accepting that this is going to take a while. You have to keep in mind how long you have been practicing your old habits. This is going to take time. Accept it and let go of having to achieve.

It is not enough that you are thinking that you are letting go. Neither is it enough just to write it down. Letting go is a physical action that your body will reward you with when it comes from within—with every cell in your body.

Find a really good reason

It is of the utmost importance that we know why we even want to change anything about ourselves or our lives. If we do not know why, then we will soon become distracted and lose focus. As soon as the going gets tough, it hurts a little, or we face a challenge, we will pull out and return to the old. We need to know why and the value of reaching that goal must be higher than ourselves.

We are in Esbjerg for a weekend seminar, at which I am teaching the students of the local club in tai chi chuan. We are taking a break, and most people are sitting along the walls, resting after a long day's practice. Daniel, one of my students, and I are standing a bit off from the others and he mentions that he would like to lose some weight and he had heard that I have helped others do the same.

Torben: *Why do you want to lose weight, Daniel?*

Daniel: That should be pretty obvious.

Torben: That is true, but why do you really want to lose weight?

Daniel: To feel better. To have a healthier life and a better constitution.

Torben: Okay, very well, but how many years have you been overweight?

Daniel: Almost my entire life. And I am 24 years old today. I weigh 124 kilos and have been through a number of diets that didn't work out. Or they did for a while, but soon after I had gained it all back—plus a little extra. I have tried just about everything and experienced failure after failure, so I am losing faith that anything really works.

Torben: That's understandable. And now I am asking you again: Why do you want to lose weight?

He looks at me strangely, as if I didn't understand Danish.

Daniel: I have told you.

Torben: But those reasons haven't worked out for you, so if you really want to lose weight and hold it, the value of doing the job and reaching the goal must be higher than yourself.

He again looked at me as if I just fell down from the moon…

Torben: If the value isn't higher than yourself, then you will lose focus as soon as the going gets tough. As soon as you face challenges. As soon as you meet temptation, as you surely will. And then the bad excuses to skip exercise or eat something that will make you gain weight will be lining up. You must think carefully about what this will mean to you, your future, those closest to you, your girlfriend, and your future kids.

All went quiet, and I could see things happening behind Daniel's eyes. He was catching on and could feel the bad conscience knocking.

Torben: Hey! You can put away that guilt. It has been with you too long and has been pulling you down. Now it will motivate you to do something about it. Accept that the past is the past. You made the choices, even if they weren't good for you. Get back in the present so we can get started.

There was no doubt that I had caught Daniel's attention. And we hadn't even noticed that all the others were listening as well.

Torben: Think about it, Daniel. And let me know if you are serious this time, because once we get started, there is no going back…

Shortly after, we started on a three-month course. Daniel lost 18 kilos in those 90 days, without strict diet. He totally changed his way of thinking and his lifestyle and lost 8 more kilos following. Daniel did it because the value of doing it was sky high. So when it got tough and challenges started appearing, they didn't come close to the value of reaching the goal.

My most important teachers: my children

When changing your habits, it's important to be motivated, but too many people wait for motivation to miraculously come upon them.

Motivation does not come by itself; it is created. I used my children to create my motivation. I could see that my children had learned some of my habits and restrictive beliefs, and I refused to let that continue. Change had to happen, and the only way I could do that was to change myself; kids do what you do, not what you say.

I realized how much my own behavior affected my children, and I would not stand by and see them continue my habits and restrictive beliefs. I did not want to see them live lives where they could not dare to be themselves; where they were afraid of making mistakes; where they are afraid to be the wonderful people they are.

My children were not aware of the importance they had on my own transformation, and they may not have done anything directly, but they have motivated me to change, to refuse to continue my behavior.

We have to change ourselves for our own sakes because we owe ourselves lives where we are faithful to ourselves, no matter what others say and think. But we must use our closest to motivate us: let the value of achieving our goals be greater than ourselves.

That's why I thank my children.

Kamilla and Daniel were born in the 90s and were only three and seven years old when I was divorced from their mother. It was sad that we could not figure it out. When I look back, I can see clearly that we did not talk about the important things. Our marriage had become superficial, and one day took another while the distance became larger between us.

I only want to tell my version and my responsibility in this development. It is clear to me today that I did not dare to be myself. I was afraid to say no, and I dared not say my opinion of fear of losing her and my family. The sad thing is that was exactly what happened, just because I did not open up and told her how I felt inside.

Did we have a chance at all? Not as it were, but if I had the strength and courage to be faithful to myself and had the courage to open up, things might have looked different today. Who knows... However, after the divorce, the children always came first. Seeing our two grown children today is a pleasure. I am a very proud father.

What motivates you?

This is, without a doubt, the most important task of all. You must know why and find the enthusiasm and obligation to do it before even thinking about how you want to do it. The "how" will come as you go along. It is easy when you know why; when you know why and know the value of doing so, there is nothing that can stop you in figuring out how.

YOUR (FUTURE) CHILDREN:

I know that I pass many of my habits on to my children. It is well known that they do not always do as I say, but more often do what I do. They see more than I can believe and copy my behavior. I know the meaning and value of letting go of the past and changing my habits. I wish to be more aware of how, for instance, I act and react when I am under pressure.

I have caught myself at reacting inappropriately, which my children paid for. I said some things too harshly, and I wish to change that. I know that doesn't happen on its own and that I can break that pattern. I know that time passes. My children will grow up and one day leave the nest no matter what I do.

Now is when I have the opportunity to affect them with my life experiences. It is my primary task—teaching them how to live a fantastic life and handle those challenges that are sure to come. Teach them to follow their hearts no matter what others might say.

I can, I will, and I am doing it NOW…

YOUR (FUTURE) PARTNER:

I know that the ones closest to me will suffer when I overreact, judge too quickly, or am afraid to lose, and I simply will not stand for that anymore. I know that I am responsible for my choices and my actions. I know that when I'm under pressure, everything inside me comes pouring out, and that it's always my partner who suffers, as she is the one closest to me.

I used to just let it be, but now it has to be different. I wish to bring everything out in the open, clean out every closet, and let go of all those old experiences that are standing in my way of becoming the absolute best partner that I know I am capable of being. I know that I am a fantastic human being, and as of today I wish to demonstrate that with my every action. The value of doing something every single day will affect not only me but everyone around me. And most importantly, it will affect my partner and our relationship. I wish to focus on listening, being an inspiration, and being thoughtful. I wish to lead by good example and not always be focused on being right, but on finding the most optimal solution for us as a couple, no matter who has that solution.

I can, I will, and I'm doing it NOW…

YOUR DREAM:

For a long time, I have had a dream of making a lot of money so I could travel. But instead of focusing on the money, I focused on the lifestyle I wanted. I focus on the experiences I want in this year. The people I wish to meet. The health I wish for, both mentally and physically, as well as the life I wish to live every single day.

Following my dreams motivates me. I set goals, plan accordingly, and nothing in me is in any doubt that I will reach those goals. I am not motivated by money but by the experience and living a fantastic life. It takes money, and that is okay. I figure out what it will take to realize my dream this year, set a date, make a plan, and 100 percent go for it.

I know that the value of living my dreams reaches far beyond myself because it affects everyone around me. I have put it to myself to be an inspiring person, and I do so by having a fantastic life and living my dreams. I wish to show other people that they can achieve everything they dream of, by doing it themselves.

I can, I will, and I am doing it NOW…

YOUR FAMILY:

My family is the most important thing in my life, that is, after myself, of course, since I need to take care of myself so that I can be there even more for my family. So everything I do for myself, everything I choose, will affect my family in one way or another.

That is why I choose to do the best for myself. And when I cannot choose the best, I choose the second best with peace of mind. I know that my way of life is no competition and that everything is perfect. I have decided to be present, inspiring, and caring. So my focus will be at being present when my family is around, to listen when they speak.

I am not on Facebook or writing texts; I am present. I want to be inspiring. Not by telling them what to do but instead showing them by doing it myself. I am considerate by being there for them when they need it. I do not worry, but pay attention to and show an interest in their lives.

I can, I will, and I am doing it NOW…

Why let go of something now?

If you have the choice of doing it now or later, do it now. In the world of the tai chi warrior, it would be disastrous to choose later. As one cannot travel back in time, I might never have another chance, so I choose to do it now.

When I look at or even just think of my children, I would never be able to justify waiting until later. It is now that I have one of the most important tasks of my life, and I will not postpone that until tomorrow. My pattern of being afraid of making mistakes had to change immediately. That was not even up for discussion. I do not want my children to grow up with the same fear of making mistakes. I want to teach them that mistakes are equal to education. I know I have to let go of the past and work diligently on changing my habits and my mindset. The value of doing so is enormously high.

EXERCISE
"How to find the motivation?"

Start by asking yourself, "On a scale of 1 to 10, how important is it for me to change this pattern/habit now?"

If that number isn't 10, then you are, most likely, not properly motivated. This demands that you have to find even more and better reasons for your next change. Those are the ones you will figure out on the next page.

Complete these sentences and repeat them for each pattern or habit you wish to change:

The pattern or habit I wish to change is:

_____

I want this because:

_____

_____

IF I CHANGE THIS, WHAT POSITIVE CONSEQUNCES WILL IT HAVE FOR:
- Me?
- My family?
- My (future) partner?
- My (future) children?
- My dreams?

IF I DO NOT CHANGE THIS, WHAT NEGATIVE CONSEQUENCES WILL IT HAVE FOR:
- Me?
- My family?
- My (future) partner?
- My (future) children?
- My dreams?

SUMMARY

We can go wherever we want, as long as we are here.

In essence, when we are here, meaning in the present, we can move in whichever direction we wish to, without old convictions of the past holding us back. We can let go of past experiences and acknowledge that what we do with the future is our responsibility.

What is it that holds you back?

Once we become aware of not doing what we know we must, in order to create the life we dream of, we have to examine and find whatever is holding us back. Is it the fear of failing, the fear of loss, or something entirely different? We need to be inquisitive and invest time in ourselves.

What did we have to learn?

We need to find out what we were to learn from the experiences of the past. What was it they wanted to teach us? What did we choose to learn? And what was the deeper meaning? Look for more experiences throughout your life in which you were in more or less the same situation. If that is the case, then look to see if the deeper meaning was the same, in which case you know what you were to learn.

I accept responsibility for my part in this.

No matter what we have been through, it is our own responsibility, no matter what meaning we give this experience. It is our own responsibility to decide how much room we allow it to take up and what value it has to have for us further on in our lives. We can choose to let it limit us or we can acknowledge that it is our responsibility to let go and create the life we dream of, without letting old convictions hold us back.

We must always know why.

Once we have set forth to change something in our lives, no matter what it is, it is important that we know why we want to do it. It is so easy to become distracted, especially when it becomes "difficult" and we face resistance, because we will. We encounter resistance from others who do not agree with us, and we will meet the resistance in ourselves when we create changes. So we need to know why we want to do this right now. It will help us to keep focus on the goal.

The value of reaching the goal must be higher than ourselves.

The more value we put into it, the more we will fight to get there. If we are "only" doing it for ourselves, it becomes easier to quit, but if the value of our changes will affect everyone around us, then the value of reaching that goal becomes larger than ourselves. And that will help us keep focus when encountering resistance and challenges.

Patience and confidence is the key to the treasure.

We must be patient in the process. It will take time. It will take the rest of our lives. It is the way and the final goal that is important. So we need to live in the present, live life as the one we truly feel that we are, and have confidence in the process and ourselves. We have been practicing our old convictions for several years, so be patient with yourselves, have confidence in yourself, and practice every day, then you cannot avoid developing in the direction you dream of.

Bring more focus on how you appear than how quickly you improve.

Let go of how fast you are developing and have focus on facing each day as the true you. Once you are aware of who you are and show it every single day, you cannot avoid reaching your goal. You cannot even avoid living as the one you truly feel you are if you practice being that one every single day.

You deserve it all. The choice is yours.

I know that is not easy to change habits and convictions. But it is not necessarily hard. It takes focus, practice, and patience. On the other hand, it will be worth it all. Once you let go of your past experiences and figure out what you were supposed to learn, acknowledge your responsibility, and let go, there are no limitations for what you may achieve. I also know that you will face resistance and challenges on your way.

What helped me was having a partner on my way. Sort of like a "no excuses coach." No matter if it is a professional or a friend, the most important thing is that they do not accept your excuses and explanations for not practicing daily. The first year we had a regular talk once a week, and in the second year once a month—it was all worth it.

It is important that you have support and understanding at home. Inform those closest to you about what you are doing, and even if they don't agree, ask them to support you anyway. If they do not wish to support you, you need to contemplate whether you need a break from them. Otherwise it will be too much of an uphill struggle for you. However, my experience tells me that those that love you will support you 100 percent, no matter if they agree with your choices or not.

I wish you all the best of luck in your way to a life free from negative past experiences. You deserve the very best in life, and it is right in front of you. Have confidence in yourself, listen to your body, be true to your heart, and never stop feeling fantastic. It is a choice.

"The Way appears before the One that follows the heart."

READY FOR BATTLE!

I know that I am the best and that I will win. Or am I the best? The doubt comes calling, but yes, of course, I am the best; I am the absolute best version of myself right now, and I am better than the others. There is now less than 24 hours until I am going in the ring, and I am filled with all kinds of emotions. I have been training seriously for this match for the past year and a half. Everything has been directed towards this match. I cannot sleep... I get up, take a walk, and get some fresh air. The coming match is running through my head. He does not have a chance. I AM the best version of myself.

Passing by a fantastic spot in the woods, I can hear the trickling stream and feel the scent of the lake in my nose. It is fantastic here, where everything is exactly as it should be—TAO (the way) I am thinking. Tao does nothing, but everything is being done; everything is perfect.

I stand and look out at the lake, let go, and sense the life around me. I assume a good broad stance and do one of my nei kung exercises, the most important exercises for my physical, mental, and spiritual balance. I let go and let the exercise take over.

Back in the hotel room, I calmly lie down and fall asleep. It is 6:00 a.m., and it is time. Well...I still have plenty of time, but I know that in order to get the optimal day, it always starts with nei kung. After a good hour, it is time for a good solid breakfast and then off to the arena. It is going to be a good day, a fantastic day, and I am really looking forward to it.

I am well balanced and ready for battle. I have done everything I could. Spent all my knowledge to create the most optimal conditions. I am at my best physical and mental shape. I am ready. I am the best. He does not stand a chance.

This is it! The excitement rises, and I am ready. We are being called to the ring. He looks strong, but I am stronger, and I can see it in his eyes that he knows—victory is mine. NOW is the time to forget everything and just be present. I close my eyes and let go of the thought of victory, let go of the thought of being the best, and let go. I am 100 percent present in the moment—I AM HERE.

He attacks right away. I dodge several times without trying to counter but wait for him to reveal his techniques. I am reading him, getting to know him without him knowing me. I am one with him; I am here. He hits me and gets ahead on the scoreboard, but that is alright because I know him without him knowing me...

Now it is time. I start countering and use his force and techniques against him. His attacks disappear into nothingness. I turn his force against himself and score one point after another. I do not register the score; I am present, and I am a 100 percent HERE. I am present and registering everything happening now, reacting freely and naturally... Everything is exactly as it should be; everything is perfect—TAO.

The match is over. It was good match. A fantastic match. I am proud of who I am.

HOW TO LEARN WUDANG TAI CHI CHUAN

There is nothing like Wudang tai chi chuan.

If you want balance and peace of mind in your life, Wudang tai chi chuan is a fantastic method. I have trained and studied these amazing Chinese movements since 1990. When I start my day with these energizing exercises, the foundation is set—the physical well-being and the mental clarity that I gain is worth gold to me in my everyday life.

The best option is no doubt to find a good master who can teach you, but if this is not possible, I have the second best opportunity for you. Through videos, I can visit you in your living room and teach you when it suits you.

I have made an online membership club where you can access a lot of videos for Wudang tai chi chuan and qigong for a very small amount as long as you are a member. Can you learn it without an instructor? Yes. I teach you when it suits you. It's true that I cannot correct your techniques, but

I have a method that I have been using for over 25 years, and I can teach you that method.

All of the videos are step by step, and I show each and every technique from multiple angles so you can get as much as possible. I have recorded the videos in such a way that it's as if I'm standing in front of you and you just have to follow along.

Learn Wudang tai chi chuan and qigong when it suits you. Find more information at: *www.TorbenRif.com/TaiChiOnline*

THANKS

A special thanks to my parents, Karen and Mogens Rif, who were always there for me. You gave me a solid foundation on which to build and were always there for me when I needed it. You have not always agreed with my choices, but you have always supported me, no matter what—for that I am deeply grateful.

Thank you to my brothers, John and Peter, for always supporting me 100 percent, no matter what I choose and no matter whether you agree with me.

Huge thanks to my master who, for better and for worse, has been my primary teacher of Wudang tai chi chuan since 1990. Dan, I am deeply grateful that I have been able to be your student for so many years and for the knowledge that you have passed on to me. You—in your own unique way—have inspired and challenged me to choose what kind of person I want to be.

I have had several coaches, instructors, and advisors during the past 30–40 years. Some I have met face to face, others through books and videos. They have all, each in their own way, inspired me to find my way.

A very special thank you to Jesper Sylvester from INFLUENCE; without his assistance, this book would never have hit the shelves. Thank you so much for your help, your humor, and your dedication. I'm looking forward to working on several projects with you in the future.

My very most important teachers through life have been and still are my children and my students, who, without being aware of it, are teaching me every single day. Thank you for the challenges you have presented me, and thank you for inspiring me to give it my best. I am deeply grateful and feel privileged to be part of your lives.

ABOUT THE AUTHOR

In 1994, Torben Rif opened his own alternative clinic giving treatments in acupuncture and massage. At the same time, he taught Wudang tai chi chuan. In 2000, he closed the clinic in order to fully commit to his teaching business, which has spread throughout Europe.

Torben has won three gold medals at the European championships in 2000 and 2008, and several of his students have become Danish, British, Dutch, Scandinavian, and European champions of tai chi.

Torben has made it his mission to help others to let go of their pride and be free of their egos, that they might find their inner selves, find strength to be true to themselves, and create the lives they dream of.

LET GO

I instruct others through workshops, lectures, mentoring, and online seminars, through which we seriously clean out before rebuilding. We become aware of where we are in relation to where we wish to go as well as discover what is holding us back. See *www.TorbenRif.com*

KEYNOTES

I give lectures at businesses in which the starting point is the tai chi warrior. It could be topics like being the best, being present, being mindful, crisis and stress handling, etc. All this combined with exercises from the world of the tai chi warrior. See *www.TorbenRif.com*

INSTRUCTOR EDUCATION

I teach and educate tai chi and qigong instructors through intensive seminars, at which my main focus is development, both of the movements and of personal development. The seminars are being held at both Vejle and in Copenhagen. See *www.ptcc.dk*

TEACHING FOR EVERYONE

I teach tai chi and qigong all around in Denmark and Europe. One of my absolute highlights is our five-day tai chi and qigong summer camp, at which we truly get in depth both theoretically and practically. See *www.ptcc.dk*

ONLINE MEMBERSHIP

I teach online in both tai chi and qigong through my online memberships, at which you as a student have access to everything I teach. It is for beginners, advanced students, and instructors alike. See *www.TaiChiOnline.dk*

INSTRUCTIONAL MATERIAL

I have published several books and DVDs about tai chi chuan, both for beginners and advanced students. See *www.TaiChiShop.dk*

www.TorbenRif.com

CPSIA information can be obtained
at www.ICGtesting.com
Printed in the USA
LVHW08s1802250918
R13954100001B/R139541PG590862LVX1B/1/P